Attitudes of Colonial Powers Toward the American Indian

Attitudes of Colonial Powers Toward the American Indian

HOWARD PECKHAM
CHARLES GIBSON
Editors

University of Utah Press
Salt Lake City

Volume Two of the University of Utah
publications in the American West,
under the editorial direction of
A. Russell Mortensen,
the Western History Center.

Preface

Nearly all history is implicitly comparative, for historians have in the backs of their minds experiences and images of other cultures or nations, or of the present, by which they measure and judge the past. So all statements about the unusual qualities or the uniqueness of a set of cultural or national traits suggest a comparison that is never really acknowledged. It has been the hope of those students interested in comparative history that open recognition of these tacit comparisons, making explicit and tangible what was formerly vague and inchoate, would enrich and deepen our understanding of the past. But comparing different cultures in different times is at best a tricky business, and historians are rightly suspicious of too facile a use of the comparative approach. Comparative history does not seem to be the same as comparative anatomy; it involves not so much general scientific principles of human behavior applicable at all times and places as an enlightenment about the ways of a particular culture at a particular time.

All of these problems of comparative history have been graphically illuminated in the continual efforts to find a common history for the American hemisphere. Yet whatever the difficulties and failures involved in the search for a general pattern in the history of the Americas, there can be little doubt that the idea of viewing the history of North and South America as a unit is still very much alive, particularly for the colonial period. While a general history of the Americas may never be written, a hemispheric focus, as Silvio Zavala has recently pointed out, does allow us "to see an over-all picture of parallel colonial experiences" that took place "during approximately the same moments in time," and "in geographic areas where some real connections were possible." By comparing the various societies and cultures of the hemisphere, "in their similarities and diversities," we can "obtain a more complete knowledge of each particular colonization and region" than we could from an isolated treatment.

It was with these thoughts in mind that the Department of History at the University of Michigan instituted its own program in comparative colonial studies. This collection of papers is one product of the initial efforts. Scholars working in particular fields of European colonization in the New World were invited to present, first in lectures at the University of Michigan and then in writing, their views of a problem common to all the American colonies—in this case the problem of transplanted Europeans confronting the Indians. None of the authors has attempted any extended comparative analysis of the topic, each confining himself to the special culture he knows best. But it is hoped and expected that the assembling and publishing of these papers will bring out questions and thoughts about the relationships between the various European colonists and the Indians that otherwise might not have been seen.

Committee on Comparative European
Colonization in America

University of Michigan

Contents

Indians and Spaniards in the New World: A Personal View

Lewis Hanke

Since I am neither an Indian nor a Spaniard, I owe the reader an explanation for describing my remarks as "a personal view." Historians rarely write or talk much about themselves or their methods. They have grander subjects to discuss, larger canvases to paint. Occasionally an Edward Gibbon tells of his moment of inspiration while contemplating the ruins of ancient Rome when he determines that his lifework will be the study of the fall of its far-flung empire, or a William H. Prescott records in his diary the long search he undertook to find a suitable subject before he decided upon the Spanish conquest of Mexico and Peru. Historians are not noted for devotion to methodology, though Hubert Howe Bancroft defended himself and his historical methods in that remarkable final volume, Number 39, which he correctly and perhaps impishly entitled *Literary Industries.* In our own time, Halvdan Koht has narrated his role in Norwegian history because he was an important part of it; J. H. Hexter has given us a blow-by-blow account of how he spends his days as a prelude to explaining why history is constantly being rewritten. But these are exceptions. Others, like Henri Pirenne and Marc Bloch, even while in prison, wrote not about themselves, but about history.

Perhaps I have been influenced in this presentation by Carl Becker and his views on *Everyman His Own Historian.*[1] Forty years

1

ago, as the most junior member of the faculty of the American University of Beirut in Lebanon, I had the audacity to write him on the subject of historical interpretations, and he had the generosity to reply wittily and at length. Afterward, I followed his writings with special interest. At a time when graduate students in history are being urged to "get with it" and learn the mysteries of the computer in order to portray the past more quantitatively, it may seem downright exhibitionistic to write about how I discovered the Indians and what an impact their relations with the Spaniards made on me, but I hope this paper will demonstrate that the subject can be approached meaningfully in this personal way; indeed, there are so many parallels between the days of the Spanish empire and our own time that new insights, or at least new approaches, are possible if we analyze those parallels.

The first contact I had with the Indians was an exhibit of arrowheads in the public library in Piqua, Ohio—a small town which I grew up in and where I began to study Spanish under a lively teacher who first roused in me a curiosity about all things connected with Spain and the Spanish language. But neither then nor in my undergraduate years did Indians of any part of the Americas particularly interest me. They were part of the scenery as the Spanish conquistadors performed their great exploits; their ancient civilizations were for archaeologists to dig up for exhibition in museums, of purely antiquarian interest. Indians were buried for me under a mass of particular facts about innumerable tribes.

Then followed my first teaching experiences at the University of Hawaii and the American University of Beirut. Let us kindly draw a veil over this four-year period—I am sure that I learned much more than my students—but these years gave me some firsthand contact with other peoples, with different cultures than that of the United States under Calvin Coolidge. Following this apprenticeship in teaching, I returned to undertake graduate work. By chance a brief but suggestive study by a Spanish scholar, Fernando de los Ríos, in the field of law and political science came to my attention and brought out the fact that many theories of government were in-

volved in the Spanish conquest of America.[2] When it became necessary to prepare a term paper for a course on the history of political
theory from Aristotle to Rousseau, I discovered that the writings of
the sixteenth-century Spanish Dominican, Bartolomé de Las Casas,
were full of ideas, and I worked out a monograph on this subject
which was limited largely to theoretical and legal aspects of Spain's
attempt to rule the Indies by just methods.[3] This approach emphasized the juridical treatises by those who preceded Las Casas (such as
Matías de Paz and Juan López Palacio Rubios), his own views, and
those of his great contemporaries of the first half of the sixteenth
century, Francisco de Vitoria and Juan Ginés de Sepúlveda. But, as I
studied more deeply the great legacy of law and political theory that
has come down to us from the sixteenth century, I began to be aware
of some of the larger problems in the interpretation of the history of
Spain in America.

The laws devised by Spain to govern her vast American dominions also formed a part of this juridical approach, for many of the
ordinances were drawn up to protect the Indians by regulating the
behavior of the Spaniards toward them. As political enemies of
Spain and others have been quick to point out, these thousands of
laws could not all be enforced throughout an empire that extended
from California to Patagonia. The phrase with which royal officials
in the New World received a new law which they did not intend to
put into effect—"Let this law be formally obeyed, but not enforced"—has become embedded in all the textbooks as a clear case of
Spanish hypocrisy. More correctly, it could be interpreted as a
means by which the execution of an unpopular or unsuitable law
could be suspended until an appeal could be made across the seas to
authorities in Spain. Of course laws were broken throughout the
enormous Spanish empire, and one of the best ways to find out what
evils the Spanish crown was attempting to abolish is by analyzing the
laws themselves. Some of the most telling descriptions of Spanish
cruelty to Indians, for example, are found in the texts of royal
orders—so much so that the seventeenth-century jurist Juan Solórzano y Pereira was ordered to remove from the manuscript of his

fundamental work, *Política Indiana*, some of the ordinances designed to prevent mistreatment of Indians so that notice of these incidents would not reach foreigners.

Laws also reflect attitudes and practices of society. Consider the significance of No. 24 of the Laws of Burgos, the first formal and detailed regulations drawn up to govern relations between Spaniards and Indians on the Caribbean island of Hispaniola only twenty years after Columbus landed: "We order and command that no person or persons shall dare to beat any Indian with sticks, or whip him, or call him dog, or address him by any name other than his proper name alone."[4] I have long suspected that some Spaniards, given their legalistic nature, must have had an Indian or so baptized with the name of *perro* (dog) so that they could call them by this name with entire legality! The laws of many peoples of course contain similar revelations. For example, the 1967 state legislature of California passed the following law: "It is unlawful to drive an automobile under the influence of glue fumes or other chemicals classed as poisons." How useful historians in future years will find this ordinance as a clue to the mores of California today!

Las Casas knew his people and their veneration for legal principles, and once said, "For forty-eight years I have been engaged in studying and inquiring into the law. I believe, if I am not mistaken, I have penetrated into the heart of this subject until I have arrived at the fundamental principles involved."[5] These fundamental principles Las Casas expounded in great, and at times painful, detail in the many treatises that I read as preparation for my study of his political theories. For this apostle, who burned with a fierce zeal on behalf of the newly discovered Indians, the true title of Spain and the only possible justification for Spain's actions lay in the donation by the pope, which was made in order to bring the Indians to a knowledge of Christ. Las Casas was bitterly scornful of the justifications which some people brought forward. To those who suggested that Spain's proximity to the Indies gave her a superior right, Las Casas pointed out that Portugal really lies closer to the New World. To those who urged the greater wisdom and understanding of Spaniards as justifying their lordship over the Indians, he replied that many other nations were wiser and of greater genius than Spain—witness the Greeks, the Africans, the Asians. To those who cited the opinion of the medieval thinker Ostiensis to the effect that all infidels are unworthy of exercising jurisdiction, he retorted that these persons do not really understand the true meaning of Ostiensis. As for those who established Spain's title because the Indians were idolatrous or committed unnatural crimes, they did not seem to realize that the Indians live for the most part an orderly political life in towns and in some respects are superior to Spaniards. And the worst reason of all was that advanced by those who justified Spain's title by her mere superiority in arms, which was an " . . . absurd, nefarious argument unworthy of being advanced by reasonable and Christian men."

Francisco de Vitoria, the Dominican professor at the University of Salamanca, never went to America, but he was also confronted with the problem of how to establish relations between Spain and the Indies. His was a more academic mind than that of Las Casas, though on many fundamental points their views coincided; in addition, he had a sense of humor, for he once remarked that if a canoe full of Indians had somehow reached Spain and "discovered" it, this fact would by no means justify Indian sovereignty over Spain. Today Vitoria is honored as one of the first and most important founders of international law, the development of which in modern times we owe to the many political theorists who sprang up in sixteenth-century Spain to argue over the true nature of her rule over the Indies.

But the legal approach is never wholly satisfactory; besides, even after the course on political theory was over, I was faced with the necessity of making "an original contribution to knowledge" in the shape of a doctoral dissertation. So in the fall of 1932, I took my wife and two small sons to Sevilla, after a summer in Germany where Adolf Hitler was beginning to reach for power with the help of his doctrine of racial superiority. In Spain I hoped to find the papers of Bartolomé de Las Casas, and, with ample documentation, to treat adequately the life of this passionate and determined friar whose influence in history has been so marked. But the papers of Las Casas—

which were so voluminous during the last few years of his life that it was difficult for visitors to get in and out of his cell in San Gregorio monastery in Valladolid—simply could not be found. After some months of desperation, I came to realize that the story I wanted to tell did not depend upon finding more Las Casas papers. His essential doctrines and ideas, for the most part, had been published. My real discovery was that he was only one, the most aggressive and articulate to be sure, of those Spaniards who sought to have the conquest follow Christian and just principles.

Therefore, during nearly two years of work in Spanish and other collections, I abandoned the plan to write about one man, Las Casas, and decided that my aim would be to demonstrate that the Spanish conquest of America was far more than a remarkable military and political exploit, that it was also one of the greatest attempts the world has seen to make Christian precepts prevail in the relations between peoples.

Since those days in the Spanish archives, my life has consisted of more study, followed by observation in the field. Sometimes these essential activities of the historian were combined. In the summer of 1935, a grant enabled me to visit Latin America for the first time to consult some original Las Casas documents in the Convento de San Felipe in Sucre, Bolivia. The Chaco War between Bolivia and her neighbor, Paraguay, was still raging, and the young German pilots in my hotel in Sucre constituted a convincing illustration of the way in which outside forces and foreign nations have so often influenced or tried to influence the course of events in Latin America. As is frequently the case, I found a manuscript I was not looking for in the convent archive. Besides the Las Casas material, there was a copy of a formal record made in Spain of the deathbed statement made by Dominican friar Domingo de Betanzos, which was related by a notary public as follows:

> In the very noble city of Valladolid on September 13, in the year of Our Lord 1549, before me, Antonio Conseco, notary public of Your Majesties, being in the monastery of San Pablo of the Order of Preachers, in a room in that monastery there was an old man with head and beard shaven, lying in bed apparently ill but in his right mind, called Friar

Domingo de Betanzos. And he handed over to me, the aforesaid notary public, a sheet of paper on which he told me he had written and declared certain matters, which concerned his conscience, and which related especially to the affairs of the Indies, which manuscript and declaration he delivered to me.[6]

This declaration referred to a written memorial Betanzos had presented to the Council of the Indies some years before in which he had declared that the Indians were beasts (*bestias*), that they had sinned, that God had condemned them, and that all of them would perish. Now on his deathbed the friar believed that he had erred " . . . through not knowing their language or because of some other ignorance," and formally retracted the statements in the memorial.

As I walked through the streets of Sucre after the archive closed for the day, I realized that for those of us interested in Latin American history the archive is not a sepulchre of dead information, but living documentation of a society much like the present. For, on my way home after my archival work had ended, I visited the ancient silver mining center of Potosí and there observed a Bolivian army officer viciously kicking Indian recruits brought together in the great Casa de Moneda for dispatch to the front. This officer also called the Indians "dogs" and other unpleasant names. Later, when philosophically-minded historians eager to split hairs denied that any Spaniard had ever called Indians "beasts" in the full scientific and philosophic sense of the word, I found it difficult to follow their subtle reasoning. I had seen with my own eyes both the retraction of Domingo de Betanzos of 1549 on his deathbed and the treatment meted out to Indians in Bolivia in 1935.

On my return to the United States, plunging into the final struggle to organize in some meaningful way the material dug out of the solid historical rock in the archives, I completed my dissertation, which had the kind of dull title too often given to academic exercises—"Theoretical Aspects of the Spanish Conquest of America."

Then in the next year I observed living Indians closely in Mexico, Guatemala, and Brazil while studying anthropology and geography after emerging from the long process of graduate study as a

7

"depression doctorate." No jobs were available since Latin American history was still considered a kind of fringe subject, and besides our universities were not expanding. Today, of course, the situation is reversed. Our newly-minted Ph.D.s kindly allow chairmen of departments and deans to compete eagerly for their services. Young scholars inquire into the fringe benefits offered and summer research grants available before they decide which position to accept. But in 1937, faced with the prospect of no job, I applied for a Social Science Research Council Postdoctoral Fellowship, and for eighteen months my family was supported while I studied cultural anthropology under the aegis of Robert Redfield and human geography with Preston James. The purpose was to broaden my interests and I was able to do so with the aid of this fellowship. Besides library study, I studied Redfield in the field as he studied the villagers in Agua Escondida above Lake Atitlán in Guatemala—a kind of parasitical existence! I discovered that this experience, brief as it was, deepened my concern for the native peoples and enlarged my understanding of the problems which the Spaniards met in their explorations. Because, in the written records of this now-distant time, Spanish voices spoke so much more loudly than those of the Indians, the historian in the Latin American field must never fail to try to hold in mind the Indian realities that were so meagerly documented, and sometimes only reflected, in Spanish records.

I had an opportunity to see how Indians and Indian problems were still of enormous concern to a number of Latin American countries, and also that present-day attitudes often influenced interpretations of the work of Spain in the New World, particularly its actions toward Indians and Indian civilization. This feeling was deepened during the twelve years I served in the Hispanic Foundation of the Library of Congress, 1939-51, a position which enabled me to travel widely in Spanish- and Portuguese-speaking lands and to discuss historical problems with their scholars. I was published rather regularly in Latin American reviews and received valuable suggestions for the improvement of my work from my colleagues. My 1949 volume on *The Spanish Struggle for Justice in the Conquest of America* was based upon my doctoral dissertation, but also reflected my experiences and discussions over a dozen years or more.

These were the days before the phrase "publish or perish" came to have such sordid connotations. Spanish-speaking historians taught me that publication was the way to express one's personality, to engage in discussion and argument with other historians in the world and thus to learn from your peers. The most regrettable result of the present "publish or perish" syndrome is not that the world has to suffer some articles and books that are too green for human consumption, but that our younger colleagues, and some older ones too, have not come to realize that unless they do let the world know what they are thinking, they will not only have no evidence to be weighed on the scales outside the dean's office, but they will cease to grow intellectually. Reluctance to write, though, is no new phenomenon. The official Spanish chroniclers of the Indies were not paid the last quarter of their annual salary until they had handed in some writing to the Council of the Indies.

My experience in the Library of Congress not only gave me an opportunity to travel widely in the Hispanic world and discuss with many scholars their ideas and their preoccupations, but also to experience the changes going on in Washington, D.C., between 1939 and 1951; many significant things occurred during this time in the nation's capital, especially concerning racial matters. One of my secretaries for a time was a young Negro whose husband was a lieutenant in the army. The Library cafeteria was opened to Negroes, and I still remember my sense of adventure when the late Professor E. Franklin Frazier of Howard University had lunch with me there. One day I noticed that a Negro was eating in the Methodist Cafeteria, opposite the Supreme Court, and discovered that this excellent eating place had been desegregated without fanfare. So I invited my old friend from graduate school days, Professor Rayford W. Logan, then Chairman of the History Department at Howard University, to lunch with me there. He had not heard of the quiet revolution at the Methodist Cafeteria, but characteristically accepted, remarking that if any difficulty arose he would speak French so that he could pass as a Haitian diplomat.

All these experiences naturally affected the way I looked at the Spanish struggle for justice in America. Now this struggle on behalf of justice for the Indians appeared to have a more universal significance than before. This feeling was reinforced on our removal to Texas in 1951 to reenter the academic world. Those were the days when the United States government and foundations alike had apparently forgotten Latin America and poured millions of dollars into the study of other areas of the world. There was some advantage in this poverty for one had an opportunity to think.

Texas, moreover, was a stimulating place to be in the decade 1951-61. This southwestern state was searching its soul on the question of justice for Negroes, and the regents of the University of Texas admitted Negroes before the Supreme Court required them to do so. But the power and the rigidity of the social structure, which had for so long maintained segregation, helped me to understand the bitter battles Las Casas fought. His intemperance alienated many in his own time and later too. His vehemence, his exaggeration, his unwillingness to sugar-coat the pill of his continuous and unpalatable criticism, and his incorrigible habit of speaking his mind freely to king, courtier, or conquistador, roused much resentment. His central idea was itself shocking to many of his contemporaries.

As I observed the events of the ever increasing battle over civil rights in Texas—for those of Mexican origin as well as for Negroes— the sixteenth century seemed to me to be drawing steadily closer to our own time. It was no superficial notion, but a fact that the social turbulence aroused then by the question of justice for the Indians had an important connection with the world situation today. In particular, I saw this with respect to the confrontation at Valladolid in 1550 and 1551 between Las Casas and Sepúlveda over the application of Aristotle's doctrine of natural slavery to the Indians.[7]

Some controversies over men and ideas of the past are no more relevant to men today than the famous medieval disputes over the number of angels that can be accommodated on the head of a pin. But the struggle for justice between men of different races and cultures, which Las Casas and other Spaniards of the sixteenth century waged, was of a different order; it concerned the fundamental challenge that Europeans had to meet when they first encountered men of different cultures and different religions on American soil in

10

that tremendous chapter of history known as the expansion of Europe. Viewed in this perspective, the Valladolid dispute lives on principally because of the universality of the ideas on the nature of man which Las Casas enunciated. He set forth, in dramatic and compelling fashion, his doctrine that " . . . all the peoples of the world are men," and his faith that God would not allow any nation to exist, " . . . no matter how barbarous, fierce, or depraved its customs," which might not be " . . . persuaded and brought to a good order and way of life, and made domestic, mild, and tractable, provided the method that is proper and natural to men is used; namely, love, gentleness, and kindness."

One of the finest passages in the Valladolid argument of Las Casas serves to illustrate the simple grandeur of which he was capable at his best:

> Thus mankind is one, and all men are alike in that which concerns their creation and all natural things, and no one is born enlightened. From this it follows that all of us must be guided and aided at first by those who were born before us. And the savage peoples of the earth may be compared to uncultivated soil that readily brings forth weeds and useless thorns, but has within itself such natural virtue that by labor and cultivation it may be made to yield sound and beneficial fruits.[8]

Las Casas was here arguing against Aristotle, but he was also stating a proposition which has rallied men in many parts of the world. He was basing his argument on the belief that the way to civilize any people was to bring religion and education to them rather than just accustoming them to the material goods they had previously not known. The recommendation of Bernardo de Gálvez in eighteenth-century Mexico that Indians were to be given " . . . horses, cattle, mules, guns, ammunition, and knives," and were to be encouraged to " . . . become greedy for the possession of land," would have been an anathema to Las Casas.

Las Casas may have been wrong in his bold declaration that " . . . all peoples of the world are men," if this is taken to mean equality in all things. Recent scientific investigations demonstrate that, on the contrary, men vary greatly in many of their physical and psychological characteristics. But few today can be unmoved by his affirmation that " ... the law of nations and natural law apply to Christian and gentile alike, and to all people of any sect, law, condition, or color without any distinction whatsoever," or by the words in which he set forth the sixth reason for the composition of his *History of the Indies*:

> To liberate my own Spanish nation from the error and very grave and very pernicious illusion, in which it now lives and has always lived, of considering these people to lack the essential characteristics of men, judging them brute beasts incapable of virtue and religion, depreciating their good qualities and exaggerating the bad which is in them. These peoples have been hidden away and forgotten for many centuries, and [it has been my purpose] to stretch out our hands to them in some way, so that they would not remain oppressed as at present because of this very false opinion of them, and kept permanently down in the darkness.[9]

At a time when the conquistadors were bringing to the notice of the European world a whole new continent inhabited by strange races, it was Las Casas, rejecting Sepúlveda's view that the Indians were an inferior type of humanity condemned to serve the Spaniard, who "stretched out his hand" to the American Indians with faith in the capacity for civilization of all peoples. This conviction, in Las Casas and other Spaniards, and the action which flowed from it, gives a unique distinction to the Spanish effort in America. Las Casas represents both that "authentic Spanish fury" with which Spaniards confront human and divine matters, and the typical attitude of the Salamanca school of sixteenth-century theologians, who believed that thought and action must be so intimately fused that they cannot be separated and that spiritual truth must be made manifest in the world about us. Las Casas thought that the end of the world might not be far off—indeed, he wrote his *History of the Indies* in order to explain God's action in the event that He decided to destroy Spain for her misdeeds in America—but meanwhile there was work to be done in the world. He would have agreed perfectly with the seventeenth-century Puritan, Matthew Henry, who declared: "The sons and daughters of heaven, while they are here in the world, have something to do about this earth, which must have its share of their time and thoughts."[10] He would also have considered as one of his followers Thomas Jefferson, who wrote a few days before he died on July 4, 1826, " . . . that the mass of mankind has not been born with saddles on their backs, nor a favored few booted and spurred, ready to ride them legitimately, by the grace of God."[11]

In an attempt to put the sixteenth-century struggle between Las Casas and Sepúlveda in perspective, I wrote a small book, *Aristotle and the American Indians*. In it I tried to show the relevance of this struggle to the present travail of our epoch of history, which might be called the expansion of the world, resulting, paradoxically, from the contraction of the world because of improved transportation and communication.

The passion aroused in Spain and America more than four centuries ago over the establishing of proper relations between peoples of different colors, cultures, religions, and technical knowledge, has a contemporary and poignant ring. Sepúlveda and Las Casas still represent two basic, contradictory responses to the culture clash resulting from the encounter between peoples who differ in important respects from one another, particularly in the *power* they hold. The hostility of those who have power toward those who can be called inferior because they are different—because they are *others*, the *strangers*—has been a historical constant. Indeed, at times it seems to be the dominant theme in human history. The challenge in our time is not only geopolitical and ideological on the international front, but touches us closely within our own society, where the cry for justice is uttered by embattled minorities who are articulate as the Indians of Latin America never were—or at least never were so far as we know from the records of history.

Today, because we North Americans hold so much power, we are beset by its consequences. The restlessness in many societies of the dispossessed, the disadvantaged—and our attitudes toward strangers, the ones who are different—has stirred in us an uneasiness because of those who now question our behavior. Sepúlveda has many followers who do not know that they follow him in believing that differences mean inferiority. So does Las Casas have followers who are deeply troubled because they believe that all the peoples of the world are men, with the rights and just claims of men, and that they must work to forward justice at home and internationally.

In November 1967, I attended the III Latin American Conference on Political and Social Sciences at the University of Santo Domingo. Of all the troubled lands of Latin America, Santo Domingo is perhaps in the most difficult situation; it suffered for thirty years under the dictatorship of Generalissimo Trujillo, and, in April 1965, was invaded by United States troops. The marks of those tragic events are still to be seen in Santo Domingo, in the minds of men as well as in the bullet holes which scar buildings there. The hostility of most conference delegates and of apparently all the student body to practically everything from the United States and to the vestiges of Spanish colonial rule was very marked. Many of the university buildings were festooned with "Go Home, Yankee" and "Down with American Imperialism" signs. Speakers at the afternoon session of November 27 could scarcely be heard, even with the aid of loudspeakers. Just outside the meeting hall, students kept up a steady barrage of slogans and rhythmic hand clapping, broken only by the ceremony of burning the United States flag and by periods of reading passages from the writings of Mao Tse-tung and Lenin.

As a historian, I could not forget that on the Sunday before Christmas in 1511, a Dominican friar named Antonio de Montesinos preached a revolutionary sermon in a thatched-roof church on the island of Hispaniola, now called the Dominican Republic. Speaking on the text, "I am a voice crying in the wilderness," Montesinos delivered the first important and deliberate public protest against the kind of treatment being accorded the Indians by his Spanish countrymen. This first cry on behalf of human liberty in the New World was a turning point in the history of America, and, as Pedro Henríquez Ureña termed it, one of the great events in the spiritual history of mankind.

The sermon, preached before the "best people" of the first Spanish town established in the New World, was designed to shock

14

and terrify its hearers. Montesinos thundered, according to Las Casas:

> In order to make your sins against the Indians known to you I have come up on this pulpit, I who am a voice of Christ crying in the wilderness of this island, and therefore it behooves you to listen, not with careless attention, but with all your heart and senses, so that you may hear it; for this is going to be the strangest voice that ever you heard, the harshest and hardest and most awful and dangerous that ever you expected to hear. . . . This voice says that you are in mortal sin, that you live and die in it, for the cruelty and tyranny you use in dealing with these innocent people. Tell me, by what right or justice do you keep these Indians in such a cruel and horrible servitude? On what authority have you waged a detestable war against these people, who dwelt quietly and peacefully on their own land? . . . Why do you keep them so oppressed and weary, not giving them enough to eat nor taking care of them in their illness? For with the excessive work you demand of them they fall ill and die, or rather you kill them with your desire to extract and acquire gold every day. And what care do you take that they should be instructed in religion? . . . Are these not men? Have they not rational souls? Are you not bound to love them as you love yourselves? . . . Be certain that in such a state as this, you can no more be saved than the Moors or Turks.[12]

The struggle that began in Santo Domingo continues today in that same troubled land, in all America, and throughout the world. The confusion over what constitutes justice and how to achieve it is also still with us, and historians still disagree sharply over their interpretations of the work of Spain in America. I still remember vividly the challenge hurled at me by a Spanish priest as I concluded a series of lectures[13] on Las Casas in Havana in 1950—a verbal challenge, for he wanted to arrange a three-day debate between us, with secretaries present, on Spanish-Indian relations. And I also remember the tremendous denunciation of Las Casas by the ninety-five-year-old Spanish scholar, Ramón Menéndez Pidal, in 1963.[14]

A totally different view was recently expressed by students in an undergraduate course at the University of Minnesota on "Man's View of his World, 1400-1800, and Now," conducted by John Parker, who reports thus on one part of their readings:

15

We read *The Spanish Struggle for Justice in the Conquest of America*, and we talked about the world as a field for Christian mission as it appeared to men of faith in earlier centuries. We discovered how much has been forgotten about the debate that went on as to the Christian's duty to the American Indian, that in the sixteenth century men like Bartolomé de Las Casas, bishop of Chiapa, saw the civil rights problem then as one which related to both law and religion. After all, it was asked, weren't these missionary champions of the Indians showing their feeling of superiority to the Indians just as much as the enslavers of Indians, but tempering their admission of inequality with benevolence?[15]

Were the friars and the other Spaniards who sought to defend the Indians basically paternalistic? Some—indeed, many—undoubtedly were firmly convinced of the immense superiority of their religion and their culture over the Indian way of life. But Las Casas and some of the other missionaries were not bigoted superpatriots. He respected many Indian customs and composed a remarkable treatise on their culture in which he did not assume that the Indians should be measured by a Spanish yardstick, but must rather be understood within the framework of their own culture. He looked at all peoples—ancient Greeks and sixteenth-century Spaniards as well as the newly discovered New World natives—as human beings in different stages of development.

Las Casas was deeply convinced of the importance of education and therefore was particularly impressed by the meticulous attention paid by the Mexican Indians to the education of their children in the ways of chastity, honesty, fortitude, obedience, and sobriety. He cried:

> Did Plato, Socrates, Pythagoras, or even Aristotle leave us better or more natural or more necessary exhortations to the virtuous life than these barbarians delivered to their children? Does the Christian religion teach us more, save the faith and what it teaches us of invisible and supernatural matters? Therefore, no one may deny that these people are fully capable of governing themselves, and of living like men of good intelligence, and that they are more than others well ordered, sensible, prudent, and rational.[16]

To practical conquistadors and administrators, men aiming at immediate worldly goals and faced with different kinds of Indians—

and perhaps to the crown as well, jealous of all royal prerogatives—Las Casas' reiteration that the only justification for the presence of Spaniards in the New World was the Christianization of Indians by peaceful means alone must have seemed dangerous nonsense. One can imagine with what contempt and horror his announcement was received that Spain ought to abandon America, with all its Indians unchristianized, rather than to bring them into the fold by forcible and, to him, profoundly unchristian methods.

As historians, we must recognize that, no matter what conclusion one reaches on Las Casas or on Spanish efforts in America, the struggles for justice—though they often failed—have endowed the history of Spain in America with a unique quality which powerfully influences the researches and the teachings of all who are concerned with Latin-American affairs, whether of the past or of the present. Cannot the undergraduates in our classes, aware as never before of the imperfections of our own society, now better understand the turbulent events of the history of Spain in America? Will they not see that the aspect of Latin-American history most bitterly discussed during all the years since 1492 has been the relations between Indians and Spaniards? The Spanish conquest has been so passionately discussed for so long because it created new societies whose old problems continue to haunt them today.

Thus the conquest is the still-living past of both Spain and Spanish America. Can we North Americans, engaged in world relations and our greatest social revolution, not learn something about Latin America's tragic problems and our own by recalling the events and protagonists of the first struggle for justice in the New World?

In the almost fifty years that have passed since, as a high school boy, I saw those Indian arrowheads in the Schmidlapp Free Public Library in Piqua, Ohio, I have come to see in my studies on the Spanish empire in America the significance of the view that all history is contemporary history.

NOTES

1— Carl Becker, *Everyman His Own Historian* (New York, 1935).

2— Fernando de los Ríos, *Religíon y estado en la España del Siglo XVI* (New York, 1927).

3— Lewis Hanke, *Las teorías políticas de Bartolomé de Las Casas*, Publicaciones del Instituto de Investigaciones Históricas, no. 67, Universidad de Buenos Aires (Buenos Aires, 1935).

4— Lesley Byrd Simpson, ed., *The Laws of Burgos of 1512-1513* (San Francisco, 1960), p. 32.

5— Hanke, *Las teorías*.

6— Lewis Hanke, *The Spanish Struggle for Justice in the Conquest of America* (Boston, 1965), p. 155.

7— Lewis Hanke, *Aristotle and the American Indians* (London, 1959).

8— Ibid., p. 112.

9— Ibid., p. 113.

10— John T. McNeill, *Modern Christian Movements* (Philadelphia, 1954), p. 34.

11— Hanke, *Aristotle*, p. 114.

12— Hanke, *The Spanish Struggle*, p. 17.

13— Lewis Hanke, *Bartolomé de Las Casas; An Interpretation of His Life and Writings* (The Hague, 1951).

14— Ramón Menéndez Pidal, *El Padre Las Casas; Su doble personalidad* (Madrid, 1963).

15— "The Manifest." A Newsletter to the Associates of the James Ford Bell Library (Minneapolis, 1968).

16— Lewis Hanke, "The Dawn of Conscience in America: Spanish Experiments and Experiences with Indians in the New World," *American Philosophical Society Proceedings* (1963), 107:90.

Black Robes Versus White Settlers: The Struggle for "Freedom of the Indians" in Colonial Brazil

Dauril Alden

When I was asked to contribute a paper to this series on Indian-white relations in colonial America, I must confess that I was both fascinated and perplexed. Fascinated because I have been attracted to the comparative approach to the study of imperial problems for some years and, having some appreciation of its advantages as well as its perils, I was convinced that this topic could be fruitfully examined comparatively. But I was also perplexed because I have never pretended to be a specialist on this subject as it relates to the area of my primary research interest, colonial Brazil, and I wondered whether I could discover a topic that would have both interest and relevance to this series. After what turned out to be an excessively long period of reflection, considering the brief time I left to put this paper together, I decided that one subject that might warrant consideration here was the struggle between members of the Society of Jesus and those whom I have perhaps too generously termed the white settlers over what contemporaries referred to as the "freedom of the Indians" problem. The related controversies over Indian rights in colonial Spanish America are well known, thanks especially to the fecund contributions of one of my distinguished predecessors in this series, Professor Lewis Hanke, but Brazilian aspects of this subject have received less scholarly attention.[1] Although I would not agree with the

19

able Jesuit historian, Serafim Leite, that this persistently thorny subject was the sole reason for the unending quarrels between the colonists and the missionaries in Portugal's New World colony,[2] it is undeniable that it was one of the fundamental issues over which they were divided for more than two centuries.

The first Portuguese contacts with the indigenous inhabitants of Brazil antedated the arrival of the Jesuits by nearly half a century. The earliest recorded impressions of the Indians are those by Pero Vaz de Caminha, secretary to Brazil's generally recognized discoverer, Pedro Alvarez Cabral. Writing the king in May 1500, Vaz de Caminha declared that the natives

> are of a dark brown, rather reddish color. They have good well-made faces . . . .They go naked . . . [and] attach no more importance to covering up their private parts . . . than they do showing their faces . . . . [He strikes a note of modernity when he adds that] one of the girls was all dyed from top to toe with that paint of theirs, and she certainly was so well made and so rounded, and her private parts (of which she made no privacy) so comely that many women in our country would be ashamed . . . that theirs were not equally perfect.

But of more vital interest to the king were the scribe's comments on the abundance of a much esteemed reddish dyewood, called brazilwood, found along the littoral and concerning the apparent willingness of the natives to assist the Portuguese in loading it aboard their ships.

> They seem to be such innocent people [he continues] that if we could understand their speech and they ours, they would immediately become Christians, seeing that, by all appearances, they do not understand about any faith . . . .I believe that if Your Majesty could send some one who could stay awhile here with them, they would all be persuaded and converted as Your Majesty desires.[3]

This optimistic, somewhat racy description of a new land and strange peoples was repeated and elaborated upon by a substantial number of visitors and sojourners who came to Brazil during the sixteenth century. But although they have a good deal to say about the political, economic, and cultural lives of the indigenous peoples with whom they came in contact, they give virtually no hint as to their

20

numbers. In the absence of materials comparable in abundance or quality to those available for a reconstruction of the population of portions of Spanish America at the time of European contact, we must be content with guestimates that Brazil's population approximated one- to one-and-a-half million in 1500.[4]

Whatever the actual number, it is evident that Brazil was one of the most sparsely occupied parts of aboriginal America and that its indigenous inhabitants were culturally and politically inferior to the advanced peoples of western South America and Middle America. The majority of the Indians with whom the Portuguese came in contact during the colonial period belonged to the Tupí-Guaraní family, and their most numerous and best-reported representatives in Brazil were the Tupinambá. In 1500 they were relatively recent occupants of much of the seacoast extending from the modern Brazilian states of Maranhão in the north to Rio Grande do Sul in the south, having displaced more primitive peoples called the Tapuia who were driven into the highland interior.

The Tupinambá were primarily root farmers who supplemented the crops they cultivated by fishing, hunting, and gathering edible fruits and nuts. Their chief staple—and that of colonial Brazil—was manioc, especially poisonous varieties, but they also grew maize, yams, sweet potatoes, beans, peanuts, peppers, plantains, and tobacco. As fishermen and boatmen they were perhaps unexcelled by any other maritime folk in aboriginal America. Wielding the long bow, they were notable hunters of wild pigs, tapirs, monkeys, armadillos, and other human beings. By the time the Europeans arrived, the Tupinambá had a well-developed tradition of constant warfare, fighting not only against their Tapuia rivals, but also against other Tupí tribes. The objects of such conflicts were primarily enemy captives who were later slaughtered with ritual and relish. The Tupinambá lived in small communities of under two thousand persons who dwelt in communal long houses clustered about a central square which served as the center of their religious and cultural life.

European observers often commented that the Tupinambá lacked "religion, laws, or kings."[5] It is true that they did not possess

monarchs and, lacking a written language, they of course had no literature or code of laws. But they did fear a variety of supernatural
forces and relied upon resident or traveling tobacco-smoking medi-
cine men (shamans, *pajes*) to protect them from misfortunes such
forces were thought capable of visiting upon them.[6]

Brazil was not formally colonized by Portugal for three decades, but it was frequently visited by explorers, ship captains seeking refuge from Atlantic storms, and, especially, dyewood hunters
called *brasileiros*. Because of the need for manpower to assist with
the felling, dressing, and loading of the wood, the *brasileiros* recruited Indian labor by means of the barter system that Portugal had
previously employed during the unveiling of the coast of West Africa, offering natives trinkets, pieces of cloth, and iron implements,
such as knives and axes, in exchange for their services.

The barter system, as Alexander Marchant has demonstrated,
worked effectively as a method of procuring labor until the Portuguese undertook formal settlements along the littoral.[7] During the
1530s and 1540s, the Portuguese government sought to promote the
colonization of Brazil by awarding portions of its coast to privileged
proprietors (captains-donatary) who were charged with the conquest, colonization, and defense of their grants. Once the settlers began to construct towns and to lay out plantations, their need for labor naturally intensified. But the Indians soon became sated with
the trade items that the settlers offered and for that reason, as well as
others, declined to continue working for them. When the colonists
resorted to attempts to enslave them, the natives rebelled, touching
off a long series of mutually destructive raids. In the end some of the
proprietors abandoned their grants; others decided against attempting colonization; still others managed to hold out precariously.[8]

By 1549 it was apparent that a more effective means of securing Portugal's rights to Brazil was imperative if she were to retain her
claim to the new land, one that several European powers were then
contesting. Thus it was that the crown dispatched a large expedition
that year to All Saints Bay under Brazil's first governor general,
Tomé de Sousa, who bore instructions to erect a fortified capital
there, to establish the rudiments of royal government, and to take

steps to strengthen existing settlements elsewhere and promote new ones.[9] Among the one thousand members of Sousa's expedition were six Jesuits, the first members of their newly founded order to be sent to the New World.

During the ensuing years—while laymen built the city of Salvador, Brazil's first capital, established plantations, and secured the Portuguese presence along the littoral extending from the captaincy of Pernambuco in the north to that of São Vicente (the future São Paulo) beyond Rio de Janeiro in the south—the Black Robes began an ambitious campaign to convert and domesticate the Indians. Initially they visited villages around the capital and near other Portuguese settlements spreading their message. "The method with which I proceed," wrote one Jesuit, "is the following: First I try to acquire the good will of the chiefs, and afterwards I discuss with them that which brought me here . . . I explain the creation of the world, the birth of the Son of God, and the Deluge, of which they have some evidence because of the tradition of their ancestors, and then I speak of the day of judgment by which many are won over because it is a thing that they have never heard of before."[10]

Although the Jesuits were soon claiming "much fruit" was being harvested during these evangelizing expeditions, they could not be sure that such fruit would long remain free from decay. To prevent neophytes from relapsing, and to protect them from hostile acts by heathen tribes and white settlers, the fathers began to gather their converts into segregated mission settlements called *aldeias*. In such settlements, as well as in the native villages and on the plantations of laymen where Indians resided, the padres attempted to root out some of the natives' most cherished traditions, including those of making war against their enemies, the consumption of captives, reliance upon the powers of wizards, drunkenness, and polygamous unions. In some instances they succeeded in persuading husbands to surrender their extra wives and to go through a marriage ceremony with their first spouse, though it was seldom easy to determine which wife actually enjoyed seniority. But it proved far more difficult for the Jesuits to persuade the Indians to abandon their other traditions.[11]

From the beginnings of their activities in Brazil the Black Robes also faced another set of problems that the white settlers posed. One that especially disturbed them was the propensity of Portuguese males to consort illicitly with native women. "In this land," wrote Father Manoel da Nóbrega a few months after his arrival in Bahia, "there is a great sin which is that almost all the men have taken Indian women as concubines ... but all make excuses ... [saying] that they do not have their [lawful] wives with them."[12] That this situation was common enough wherever Europeans went overseas in these times did not make it any less reprehensible from the standpoint of the Jesuits who, as they visited communities up and down the coast, pointed their finger at profligate Portuguese colonists and urged royal authorities to compel them, if single, to marry their native paramours, or, if already married, to send home for their wives. In time, as the Indian population dwindled and as the number of eligible white women increased, concubinage became less of a social problem along the seacoast, though it continued to exist in the more sparsely settled parts of Brazil for centuries.

Another problem that confronted the Jesuits from the start and that continued to do so as long as they remained in the colony was that of the whites' enslavement of the Indians. Early in 1550 Father Nóbrega reported:

> In this country the majority of the inhabitants have their consciences heavily weighted down because of the slaves whom they hold unjustly, besides the many ... who were purchased from their fathers and whom the inhabitants will not free. ... Thus Satan has all these souls in his power ... because the men who came out here find no other means of livelihood than by the work of their slaves, who fish and hunt food for them, and slothfulness rules them to such a degree ... that they are not disturbed at being excommunicated, provided they keep the slaves.[13]

This was the first of many Jesuit condemnations of a practice they regarded as morally wrong and as seriously jeopardizing their own efforts to persuade the Indians to lead Christian lives. But Nóbrega's protest placed Brazil's first governor general in the very dilemmas that were to confront so many of his successors in the colony and their superiors at home: Was it possible to respect the freedom of the

Indians, as the Jesuits urged, and at the same time accommodate the legitimate needs of the settlers for manual workers? If, on the other hand, the king's officers winked at the colonists' subjugation of the natives, would not the consequence be a constant succession of wars that would ultimately result in the elimination of the Europeans or the Indians? As Professor Marchant has shown, Sousa and his immediate successors worked closely with the Jesuits and tried various measures to persuade the Indians to labor voluntarily for the Portuguese and to restrict enslavement of the natives to those captured in so-called "just wars" fought against tribes that proved persistently hostile to the settlers and the missionaries.[14]

With varying degrees of success, these policies were pursued by the governors general for the next two decades. During that time the numbers of Portuguese and Negro slaves in the colony (first introduced about 1550) steadily increased, and the Lusitanians gradually extended their sway over the Atlantic littoral from the so-called hump to São Vicente, ousting French intruders and indigenous occupants who got in their way.[15] Strangely enough it was not until 1570, long after the Spanish crown issued its first legislation concerning relations between its colonists and the aborigines, that the Portuguese government enacted its first law that specifically dealt with Indian affairs. In it the king prohibited the enslavement of the natives of Brazil except for those taken in a just war—one that had been authorized by the king or his senior representative in the colony. Natives found illegally held in bondage were declared free.[16]

It is unclear whether the Jesuits were instrumental in the passage of this law, though it is likely that they were.[17] Certainly the Black Robes enjoyed great influence with the Portuguese court and with its chief agent in Brazil at this time, the memorable Mem de Sá, Brazil's third governor general (1557-72). It was during or shortly after his term that Pero Magalhães de Gandavo, the Portuguese humanist, completed the first history of Brazil. In his chronicle, Magalhães de Gandavo observed that:

> The Fathers have done many . . . beneficent and pious deeds in those
> parts, and are continuing to do so, and in truth one can not deny them

great praise. Because these deeds are so praised throughout the land, it is unnecessary for me to deal more extensively with them here: it is enough to know that their acts are . . . approved everywhere as holy and good . . . .[18]

Whether such approbation was this widespread in the colony at the time the chronicler wrote may be questioned; certainly it was far from universal a decade later when the Jesuits found themselves in a hornet's nest.

During the administration of Manuel Teles Barreto (1583-87), the Black Robes became embroiled in a series of controversies with the governor general, members of his staff, and the sugar planters of Bahia. One subject of these disputes concerned allegations that the Jesuits were responsible for an Indian massacre north of Bahia that had taken the lives of several hundred Portuguese and Indian allies. Another was a charge that the padres were illicitly keeping Indians in their missions who legally belonged to the planters. These and other complaints led to a flood of memorials to the court by the fathers and their adversaries.[19] The bearer of some of the Jesuits' opponents' complaints was none other than Gabriel Soares de Sousa.

Gabriel Soares de Sousa had been a sugar planter in Bahia since about 1570 and returned to the kingdom in the late 1580s in order to apply to the crown for a concession to exploit suspected mineral resources northwest of Salvador. He is widely known as the author of the *Descriptive Treatise on Brazil*, a work he completed during the 1580s and one that remains the most informative account of the colony written during the sixteenth century. Less generally recognized is the fact that he was also the author of a shorter work entitled "Charges that Gabriel Soares de Sousa gave in Madrid to D. Cristóvão de Moura against the Padres of the Company of Jesus . . . in Brazil," the manuscript of which was also finished during the 1580s.[20] Since Soares de Sousa found few occasions to mention the Jesuits in the *Descriptive Treatise*, where he spoke of their activities in vague but favorable terms,[21] it is rather surprising to discover the intensity of his real feelings toward them. His "Charges" are divided into forty-four observations (called "informações") which fall into three major categories: the first concerns statements that the Black

Robes had allowed themselves to become deeply involved in political intrigues in the colony; the second alleges that they had forsaken their original spiritual mission in Brazil and had become materialistically oriented; the third constitutes a detailed critique of the Jesuits' role in Indian affairs. The author poured scorn on the large number of converts that he said the fathers claimed, noting that their neophytes took the first opportunity to flee into the forests to escape the missionaries. He contended that the Black Robes visited the settlers' plantations primarily to incite legitimate Indian slaves to flee their masters, offering them sanctuary in their missions, denying the right of whites to enter the *aldeias* by threatening them with imprisonment and excommunication. He strongly intimated that the Jesuits were guilty of sinning with naked Indian maidens during the confessional and accused them of refusing to contribute native levies to assist the colonists in putting down Indian uprisings. Sousa insisted that the padres were interested in the Indians because they wished to exploit them for their own purposes, and he warned that unless the planters were assured ample supplies of Indian slaves the economy of Brazil could not survive.

A remarkable philippic—this "most anti-jesuitical document of sixteenth-century Brazil," as its discoverer Father Leite had called it—Sousa's "Charges" contains many of the allegations that were destined to be repeated for centuries by the Jesuits' opponents. Whatever one may wish to think of their merits, Sousa's accusations obviously reflected longstanding grievances, real or imagined, among the settlers of early Brazil.[22] And since they were addressed to such an important personage as Cristóvão de Moura, Philip II's chief adviser on Portuguese affairs,[23] they had to be answered. The Jesuits realized as much and assembled a committee of leading Black Robes in Salvador to do so. Its members included the provincial, two former provincials, the procurator, a secretary of the former visitor general to Brazil, Fernão Cardim, himself a notable treatiser on Brazil, and the distinguished historian, linguist, and missionary, José de Anchieta. In their point-by-point refutation of Sousa's "Charges," the committee found opportunity to inject some sharp jibes at their author, but admitted that in their efforts to protect the Indians

27

against enslavement, disposal by sale, and branding, "the Padres have many against them in the colony."[24]

The Jesuits' reply was signed in 1592. By then the Black Robes seem to have weathered this particular storm. Manuel Teles Barreto, the most hostile governor general they encountered during the sixteenth century, and Gabriel Soares de Sousa, in the end a frustrated prospector, had already passed to their ultimate rewards. Three years later, in 1595, the crown issued a second law concerning the enslavement of the Amerindians that further narrowed legal grounds for just wars against the natives.

Three further statutes were added at the beginning of the seventeenth century, the first two very favorable to the Jesuits' position on Indian freedom, the third distinctly less so. A decree of 1605 declared that

> in no case may the natives of Brazil be taken captive, even though [in the past] there may have been some legal justifications for such seizures, those to the contrary [are] of so much greater consideration, especially those pertaining to the conversion of the natives to our Holy Catholic Faith, that these . . . must be placed before all the rest.

Four years later another royal edict declared that both Christian and pagan Indians were born free and remained so under the law; consequently they could not be compelled to render service against their will and must be compensated for any labor they provided. As was the case in the 1570 law, natives held against their will were declared free, but this time violators were threatened with punishment for the crime of enslaving free persons.

It is easy to speculate that the Jesuits had a hand in the drafting of these laws, but the fact is that we simply do not know what role they may have played in their formulation. Evidently the new laws aroused bitter complaints on the part of the settlers, for two years later their provisions were significantly modified. The law of 1611 contained three important provisions: (1) It again sanctioned the principle of just war under certain circumstances; (2) it declared that settlers who had ransomed Indian captives presumably intended for cannibalistic feasts were entitled to compensation in the form of ten-years labor for each captive they liberated; and (3) it authorized the appointment of lay captains—i.e., married settlers—instead of Jesuit missionaries as the overseers of the temporal affairs of Indian communities.[25]

In actuality this legislation had scant effect upon the Indians of the coastal zones originally settled by the Portuguese, for, by the turn of the seventeenth century, most of those not already living in Jesuit missions or on the settlers' estates had vanished from the littoral. Some had died off as a result of punitive campaigns waged by the Portuguese or their Indian allies; others had fallen victims to diseases of European or African origin; many had expired because of their inability to adjust to the demanding labor regime that prevailed on the plantations; still others had fled to the interior where they and their cousins were pursued by the missionaries and their rivals.[26]

But the struggle for freedom of the Indians was far from over. During the seventeenth and eighteenth centuries it was fought out primarily along the vast stretches of the interior in the far south and far north of Brazil, areas where, significantly, the authority of the crown was weakest and where the position of the Black Robes was most exposed. In the south, beginning in the 1590s, hordes of explorer-slavers—many of them more familiar with the Tupí tongue than with their own native Portuguese, many of them in fact part blooded Indians (*mamelucos*), and all of them heavily indebted to Indians for their modes of dress, cuisine, forms of transportation, and fighting equipment—spilled over the Luso-Spanish frontier in their quest for Indian slaves.[27] Between 1628 and 1641 these marauding *bandeirantes*, as they were called, overran and destroyed two mission fields west and south of the town of São Paulo that had been recently founded by Jesuits based in Spanish Paraguay. They succeeded in carrying off thousands of neophytes who were sold to planters along the littoral, and they were prevented from doing further damage only after they met armed resistance from Jesuit-led Guaraní warriors. Then the *bandeirantes* turned their attention to other parts of the continental interior, searching for both human and material resources to exploit.[28]

Although these raids did not directly affect lands where Portuguese Jesuits were actively engaged in missionary work, the Jesuits nevertheless strongly condemned them. But when Jesuits in São

Paulo and in Rio de Janeiro attempted to invoke the authority of Pope Urban VIII, who in 1639 issued a bull reiterating the century-old papal dictum forbidding enslavement of Amerindians on any pretexts, they met stiff opposition from the colonists. In São Paulo the settlers twice expelled the missionaries from their captaincy during the 1640s, while the fathers in Rio de Janeiro averted a similar experience only by making humiliating concessions to the settlers on the subject of Indian slavery.[29]

On the defensive in the south, the Black Robes took the offensive in the far north. There, beginning in the first years of the seventeenth century, the Portuguese established a series of far-from-prosperous or populous settlements from the hump to the Amazon, expelling European rivals and subjugating Amerindians who opposed them. In the 1620s this area was administratively organized as the State of Maranhão, and from then until the late eighteenth century it was separately governed from the rest of Brazil, termed the State of Brazil. The first major Jesuit undertaking in Maranhão ended tragically in 1643 when twelve of fifteen Black Robes perished indirectly as a consequence of a shipwreck.[30]

Nineteen years later the Jesuits returned to Maranhão under the leadership of one of the most remarkable men of any age, certainly the greatest figure of the Portuguese Atlantic empire during the seventeenth century, and the foremost champion of Indian freedom in Brazil during the entire colonial period. I refer to Father António Vieira, the closest Portuguese equivalent to the better known Bartolomé de Las Casas. Vieira was born in Lisbon in 1608 of partly mulatto antecedents, grew up in Brazil, where he entered the Jesuit order at an early age, and became a sometime missionary, an adviser to Portuguese monarchs, a frustrated diplomatic agent, a masterful preacher, and a remarkably acute expository writer.[31] Among the many causes that Vieira championed in his sermons and with his quill, none was more important to him than the protection and conversion of the Amerindians.

Vieira arrived in Maranhão early in 1653 and was appalled by the extent to which the Indians were being abused by the settlers and their governors. He declared that he could see no real distinction between the Indians who served as slaves on the plantations and those who were called free but were exploited by the governors and their staffs for their own gain. He urged that all private ransoming expeditions to the interior be prohibited, since he contended that they were not motivated by Christian charity but by pure greed. In the future, he said, such expeditions ought to be undertaken solely to convert the heathen and to reduce them to Christianity. He also recommended that laymen be excluded from all Indian villages and that existing laws concerning Indian liberty be strictly enforced. Such policies, Vieira declared, would lead to peace in the interior and persuade the Indians to come out of the forests voluntarily to accept Christianity and remunerated employment on the plantations.[32] For their part the settlers strongly disagreed. They wrote the king that their own livelihood depended largely upon the availability of Indian workers and insisted that the benefits the natives received from their conversion were sufficient compensation.[33]

In 1655 Vieira returned to the kingdom to press for the enactment of more stringent legislation in behalf of the Indians.[34] One result of his efforts was the framing of a new law in 1655 which the king declared, wistfully one would think, definitive. Although it virtually prohibited offensive campaigns against the indigenous population, it did authorize defensive actions whenever a tribe evinced hostility against the state or opposed the spread of the gospel. It also recognized the right of persons responsible for liberating captives to five years of personal service after which the Indians were to become part of a common labor pool. Another consequence of Vieira's visit was the drafting of a new instruction for the governor of Maranhão which directed him to give priority in his actions to the dissemination of the faith and to work closely with the Jesuits who were exclusively entrusted with the task of converting the Amazonian Indians and were assigned a major role in the distribution of Indian workers to the settlers.[35]

In spite of having achieved only part of his objectives, Vieira returned to Maranhão, very much aware of the fact that the days ahead might well be perilous for the Black Robes. He was convinced that the settlers would make use of every opportunity provided by the new law to continue their efforts to enslave Indians, and he realized that the dominant position assigned to the Jesuits in the region made them vulnerable to attacks on all sides. He wrote:

> We have against us the people, the[other] religious [orders], the proprietors of the captaincies, and all those in the Kingdom and in this State who are interested in the blood and sweat of the Indians whose inferior condition[*menoridade*] we alone defend.[36]

In the following years he repeatedly begged the king to stand firm in upholding the law of 1655 and to give exemplary punishments to those who thwarted it, for in language reminiscent of Las Casas he declared:

> The injustices and tyrannies that have been practiced on the Indians of these lands exceed by far those that have been perpetrated in Africa. In the space of forty years . . . more than two-million Indians and in excess of 500 Indian settlements, [some] as large as cities, have been ravaged without any punishments[having been meted out] for such misdeeds.[37]

Such criticism did not endear Vieira and his colleagues to the settlers. The climax of several years of mutual recriminations came in 1661-62 when the citizens of the two most important towns in the State, São Luís and Belem, revolted and shipped the Black Robes back to the kingdom.[38] For their defiance of the will of the reigning monarch, the colonists later received a general pardon.[39]

Vieira tried to secure the court's support for the return of the Black Robes to Maranhão upon his arrival in Lisbon, but was thwarted by a palace revolution that found him backing the losing side. Subsequently he was harassed by the Inquisition and spent a decade of voluntary exile in Italy. When he came back to Portugal in 1679, Vieira renewed his campaign in defense of Indian freedom. The fruits of his efforts were the enactment of a new series of laws intended to protect the Indians and the restoration of the Jesuits in Maranhão. The most important of the new laws, that of April 1, 1680, unequivocally prohibited future enslavement of the Indians, again threatened violators with severe punishments, and declared that Indians captured in offensive or defensive campaigns would thereafter be treated as prisoners of war rather than as slaves and would be assigned to Jesuit *aldeias*. The Black Robes were again given exclusive responsibility for the spiritual welfare of the Indians in the State, including the management of Christianizing expeditions to the back lands and a significant voice in the distribution of Indian workers.[40]

Although the laws of 1680 represented a major victory for the Black Robes, they inevitably produced strong adverse reactions on the part of settlers both in the far north and in the far south of Brazil. In the captaincy of Maranhão they led to the so-called Beckman revolt (1684), a protest movement directed not only against the Jesuits and the crown's new Indian policy, but also against a recently created monopoly company intended to supplement the available native labor force by supplying Negro slaves to the State.[41] Once again the Black Robes were driven from the captaincy of Maranhão (though not from neighboring Pará), and for a time the fathers contemplated abandoning the Amazonian mission field because of the crown's inability to offer them adequate protection or to enforce its legislation concerning the treatment of the Indians.[42]

But Pedro II of Portugal (1683-1706), perhaps the ablest of the Bragança monarchs, made it clear that he very much wanted the Jesuits to continue their work in the north. Besides quashing the tumult and severely punishing its ringleaders, the king restored the Jesuits to Maranhão, sent his personal assurances to their general that he was determined to support the missionaries,[43] and tried to find a permanent solution to the perennial Indian problem. In 1686, after hearing testimony from all sides, the crown issued the celebrated Maranhão missions ordinances (*regimento*).[44] A comprehensive body of legislation, the ordinances awarded the Jesuits and the Franciscans—now newly admitted to the State and subsequently to be joined by the Carmelites and Mercedarians—complete jurisdiction within their *aldeias* and strictly barred all unauthorized colonists from entering them. However, the missionaries were directed to locate future *aldeias* near the colonists' communities so as to facilitate trade and the procurement of labor. The distribution of Indian workers, their rate of pay, and the length of service they were required to perform was to be determined by the governor (or his deputy) upon consultation with the leaders of the religious orders and the municipal councils (*câmaras*) of Belem and São Luís.[45]

The ordinances of 1686 did not repeal that part of the 1680 law that forbade any enslavement of the Indians. However, that prohibition was significantly modified by a subsequent law passed in 1688. It was necessary to do so, rationalized the king, because experience had shown that there was a danger that the souls of many heathens would remain unsaved otherwise and that there was a prospect that slaves of the Indians themselves would be sold to Portugal's foreign rivals. Consequently, the crown again sanctioned slaving expeditions in particular circumstances. They were permitted when the missionaries certified that hostile tribes were preparing to attack Portuguese lands, or had invaded the property of Christians, or were inhibiting the preaching of the gospel.[46]

In many respects these new laws represented a compromise between the maximum goals of the settlers and those of the Black Robes, between unrestricted secular exploitation of the Indians and exclusive missionary control of the natives. Whether or not a "masterpiece of legislation," as one historian has labeled them,[47] the ordinances of 1686, which defined the crown's basic Indian policy in the Amazon until the turbulent 1750s, did provide a workable solution to an old and complex problem. Assuming the good will of all parties concerned and consistent enforcement by the king's agents—two dubious assumptions to be sure in the light of previous experience—they assured the Indians, the missionaries, the settlers, and the crown that their vital interests would be safeguarded. It is lamentable that the crown relented in its opposition to any form of Indian enslavement. That the Jesuits did not seriously condemn the law of 1688 at the time it was issued is indicative of the fact that by then the fathers had concluded that if they intended to continue to function in the Amazon they must compromise their principles.

The Black Robes also found it necessary to make such a compromise in another theatre, São Paulo. There, too, news of the king's decree of April 1, 1680, proscribing enslavement of the Indians, was greeted with indignation by the settlers who made menacing gestures against the Jesuits, the presumed sponsors of the law.[48] There, too, the Black Robes seriously considered ceasing all activities and actually sought their general's permission to withdraw from the captaincy. Impressed by the seriousness of the Jesuit's resolve, the Paulistas (residents of São Paulo) changed their minds, and in 1684 both the governor and the *câmara* of São Paulo beseeched the provincial to reconsider. Convinced by the sincerity of the Paulistas' pleas, the fathers decided to remain.[49]

But a new crisis developed in 1691, for in that year the king issued still another decree forbidding enslavement of the Indians and insisted that colonists who employed them must adequately compensate the Indians for their services.[50] The circumstances that prompted the issuance of this decree are far from clear. Evidently it was intended to apply throughout the State of Brazil, particularly to the captaincy of São Paulo where, according to a contemporary statement, there were an estimated eighty thousand Indians, most of them presumably considered slaves.[51] To persuade the Paulistas to observe the new law, the governor general asked the venerable Father Alexandre de Gusmão, Jesuit provincial, to proceed from Salvador to São Paulo to serve as the king's spokesman.[52] According to Gusmão's later report, he found the conviction widespread in the captaincy that "it was lawful to hunt Indians in the back lands, bringing them back in chains, putting them to work, giving them as presents, selling them, or using them to pay debts; . . . and that they said that they bring them to the bosom of the Church and give them sufficient food and clothing and that this is more than adequate compensation for their labor."[53]

After extended discussions between the leading figures of the town of São Paulo and the provincial, the latter and the officers of the *câmara* signed a curious pact. In it the Paulistas declared themselves convinced that all Indians must be considered "completely free" regardless of their origins. They promised that they would send no more slaving parties into the back lands in search of natives and that they would no longer purchase, sell, exchange, or use Indians to discharge their debts. However, wrote the signatories, since it was manifestly wrong to return Indians who had become Christianized

35

to the places of their origin, because there they would revert to their customary bestiality and be without benefit of pastors, the Indians would remain in the captaincy and work for laymen who would serve as their "administrators, tutors, and guardians."[54]

Exactly what kind of relationship ought to obtain between the Indians and their "administrators, tutors, and guardians" became the subject of a second document signed by the *câmara* and the provincial a year and a half later.[55] Entitled "Doubts Which are offered by the Settlers of the Town of S. Paulo to His Majesty and the Lord Governor General of the State concerning the Method of keeping the Agreement . . . pertaining to the Use of the Natives," it listed sixteen questions to which the colonists sought answers "for the greater tranquility of our consciences." Some of the "doubts" that troubled the Paulistas were the following: (1) If an Indian flees to Rio de Janeiro or to some other place, can he be forcibly returned to the residence of his administrator? (2) Upon an administrator's death, can the Indians he formerly supervised be divided among his sons? (3) If an Indian becomes obnoxious to an administrator's family because of his vices and bad behavior, may the administrator transfer him to the jurisdiction of another? (4) If an Indian boy under the care of one administrator falls in love with an Indian maiden who is the responsibility of another administrator, can the two administrators arrange an exchange of Indians and charge a fee to permit the couple to marry?[56]

Surprisingly enough, most of the leading Jesuits in the province—including Jorge Benci, later a critic of the treatment of Negro slaves in Brazil, and João António Andreoni, a notable anti-Semite and the writer of the remarkably informative *Wealth and Culture in Brazil* (1711)[57]—supported the provincial's belief that the pact should be accepted.[58] But one who expressed more than a few "doubts" concerning its advantages to the Indians was António Vieira. Vieira had returned to Bahia in 1681 determined to spend the rest of his days there, as he did. Although he no longer possessed the degree of influence he formerly enjoyed at court or even within his own order, the king specifically sought his advice concerning the proposed agreement.[59]

Despite the infirmities of an extraordinarily active, purposeful, and ever-contentious life, the eighty-seven-year-old father responded with an opinion (*voto*) that revealed he had lost none of his ability to express himself with remarkable lucidity, force, and incisiveness, and that he remained as uncompromising in his defense of Indian freedom as he had been nearly half a century before. Vieira began by asserting that the Indians illegally seized by the Paulistas had been "living as free and natural lords of their lands" and therefore could not be legitimately considered as slaves of the Paulistas nor even as vassals of the king. Then he raised several "scruples" concerning the proposed agreement. He observed that all of its alleged benefits would accrue to the settlers while all of the burdens would fall upon the Indians, that because the pact denied the Indians freedom of persons, of movement, and of estates, they "ought [properly] to be called captives, rather than free men," and that the sort of compensation and protection the administrators were supposed to give them was no more than a master was expected to provide his slaves. Such a regime, Vieira pointed out, had its origins in the encomienda system of Spanish America which had been condemned by many authorities, including José de Acosta and Juan Solórzano Pereira, whose *Política indiana* he quoted at length concerning the Spanish crown's legislation against forced Indian personal service. He observed that the kind of relationship between laymen and Indians envisioned in the accord was precisely that which had been repeatedly tried in Maranhão, where the so-called lay captaincies had proven in practice to be no more than a disguised form of slavery and had therefore been prohibited. Vieira concluded by urging that the proper relationship between the Paulistas and the Indians ought to be entirely voluntary, and assured the king that if the settlers treated the Indians as well as they should, they would have no difficulty in persuading them to settle near their estates and to work for them in return for reasonable compensation.[60]

Vieira's famous *voto*, signed on July 12, 1694, was destined to be his last major statement in defense of Indian freedom. Three years and six days later he was gone. Very likely he died resigned to the fact that his last efforts to protect the Indians against what he always regarded as the "avarice" of the settlers had been unavailing.[61] In fact, Pedro II, though incorporating some of Vieira's recommendations, did approve the new regime in 1696.[62]

Whatever one may think about Vieira's assumptions concerning the willingness of the Indians to serve the whites voluntarily, he was certainly correct in his contention that the Paulista administrations bore a suspiciously close resemblance to the lay-captaincy system that had been tried several times in the Amazon during the seventeenth century and had been repeatedly abolished because of its evident inequities.[63] The fact that the crown and most Jesuits in Brazil were now prepared to accept this arrangement betokens the spirit of the age of Pedro II. As far as that spirit affected the attitude of the Black Robes, it is apparent that the heroic age of Nóbrega, Anchieta, Figueira, and Vieira was passed: militancy had given way to accommodation. It is true that during the eighteenth century the Jesuits' missions in the Amazon flourished as never before, but the Black Robes' very success led to their undoing, to their definitive expulsion from all Portuguese lands in 1759.[64] Two years earlier the crown, utilizing a long suppressed papal bull in defense of freedom of the Indians that had been ironically directed specifically against the Jesuits, deprived the missionaries of control over their *aldeias* and assigned their supervision to so-called "directors," i.e., lay captains in military regalia. Thus, as they had in the south, the white settlers in the north ultimately triumphed over the Black Robes and gained supremacy over the Indians. What happened afterward lies beyond the limits of this paper. Suffice it to say that the Indians suffered disastrously, and that in 1798 the directorates, along with the Paulista administrations, were abolished.[65]

Certain conclusions emerge forcefully from the foregoing account. First, it is evident that the struggle between the Black Robes and the white settlers was rooted in their divergent objectives in the colony. The primary goal of the Jesuits was the conversion of the heathen to the true faith; the major aim of the colonists was the advancement of their own economic welfare. Both were interested in the Indian for quite different reasons: the colonist to exploit him for his labor, the missionary to remold his cultural outlook. Second, each side viewed the other's preferred methods of treatment of the Indian as inimical to the fulfillment of its own aims, and therefore each appealed to the crown for legislation to support its interests and to frustrate those of its rival. Third, the crown—beset as it was for two centuries by conflicting testimony from settlers, royal officials, Jesuits, and rival ecclesiastics concerning the kind of Indian policy it ought to follow—could never make up its mind to adhere to a consistent line of policy. Indeed, prior to the eighteenth century it usually lacked adequate means to enforce that which it elected to pursue at a particular moment. Fourth, in spite of their differences, there were certain subjects on which the settlers and the Jesuits were, in fact, in agreement. Both, for example, believed that the advancement of their interests depended upon an abundance of servile labor. Because of their experience before coming to Brazil and other considerations, both preferred Negro slaves when they were available and within their means. Indeed, one of the anomalies of the Jesuits' attitude toward *Indian* slavery was their failure to condemn *Negro* slavery, a point conceded by Father Leite but one he does not very convincingly explain away.[66] But Negro slaves were always relatively expensive in the colony, and it was precisely in those areas where the Luso-Brazilian settlers were most impoverished—i.e., in the far south and the far north—that they relied most heavily upon Indian labor; it was over the conditions that ought to govern the performance of that labor that the settlers and the missionaries repeatedly clashed. Another area where the Jesuits and the colonists found common ground was their low estimate of the cultural worth of the Amerindians. True they admired his physical courage, his knowledge of natural lore, and sometimes his manual skills, but I know of no writer, Jesuit or layman, who ever expressed any admiration for the Indian's heritage or his intellectual abilities.[67] It was because both regarded the Indian as possessing inferior mental capabilities that both adopted a paternalistic attitude toward the native. That was the theoretical justification for the lay-captaincy system and it was also a raison d'être of the mission system. Therefore, and this is my fifth and final point, the struggle for "freedom of the Indians" was not a conflict over freedom as it is defined today. Not freedom in a modern sense, but, as Father Leite himself admits, *"protective* liberty was the presupposition of all the legislation concerning Indian freedom."[68] The Jesuits thought of freedom of the Indians as connoting liberty of persons and property, but they did not concede that it included the right of natives to resist by force peaceful white penetrations of their territory, nor to reject the virtues of Christianity in favor of pagan traditions. The missionaries were as convinced as the settlers that there were circumstances where subjugation was necessary before the Indians' way of life could be fundamentally changed.[69] That it could and must be were their major premises. Rightly or wrongly, the Black Robes believed that the sort of protection they offered the Indian would safeguard him from the physical abuse and the moral depravity likely to be his fate at the hands of the settlers. Whether the Indian was significantly better off under the tutelage of the fathers than under the domination of the settlers depends upon the value system one holds and how one reads the evidence. For my own part I have no doubt that he was.

BLACK ROBES VERSUS WHITE SETTLERS

NOTES

1– A pioneer study emphasizing legal aspects of Indian-white relations, primarily in the Amazon, from colonial beginnings until 1910 is Alipio Bandeira and Manoel Tavares da Costa Miranda, "Memorial acerca da antiga e moderna legislação indigena, com um projecto de lei difinindo a situação juridica do indio brazileiro," (1911), rpr. in Alipio Bandeira, *Collectanea indigena* (Rio de Janeiro, 1929), pp. 35-71. Narrower in scope is Antonio Raiol Domingos (Barão de Guajará), "Catechese de indios no Pará," *Annaes da biblioteca e archivo público do Pará*, II (Belem, 1903), 117-83. The major bibliography of Brazilian ethnology is Herbert Baldus, *Bibliographia crítica da etnologia brasileira* (São Paulo, 1954); see also idem, "Sinopse da bibliografia crítica da etnologia brasileira, 1953-1960," *Arquivo do Instituto de Antropologia*, I (Natal, 1964), 5-22, which appears in translation in Janice H. Hopper, ed. and trans., *Indians of Brazil in the Twentieth Century* (Washington, D.C., 1967), pp. 207-28. The major English language studies of particular aspects of Indian-white relations in colonial Brazil are Alexander Marchant, *From Barter to Slavery. The Economic Relations of Portuguese and Indians in the Settlement of Brazil, 1500-1580*, rpr. (Gloucester, Mass., 1966), and Mathias C. Kiemen, *The Indian Policy of Portugal in the Amazon Region, 1614-1693* (Washington, D.C., 1954). See also, Charles R. Boxer, *Race Relations in the Portuguese Colonial Empire, 1415-1825* (Oxford, 1963), pp. 86-101, and other studies on Brazil by the same writer.

2– *História da companhia de Jesús no Brasil* (hereafter cited as *HCJB*), 10 vols. (Rio de Janeiro, 1938-1950), 6:352; see also 2:92 for a similar statement.

3– A convenient English translation of Vaz de Caminha's letter of May 1, 1500, to King Manuel the Fortunate may be found in Charles David Ley, ed., *Portuguese Voyages 1498-1663* (London, 1960), pp. 39-59. The quotations are from pp. 43, 47, and 56.

4– Charles Wagley, "The Indian Heritage of Brazil," in T. Lynn Smith and Alexander Marchant, eds., *Brazil, Portrait of Half a Continent* (New York, 1951), pp. 104-105.

5– In addition to the contemporary sources cited on this point in Capistrano de Abreu and Rodolfo Garcia, eds., *Diálogos das grandezas do Brasil* (Salvador, 1956), p. 349, n. 4, see Brother António Blázquez to the Fathers and Brothers of Coimbra, July 8, 1555, Serafim Leite, ed., *Monumenta brasiliae* (hereafter cited *MB*), 4 vols. (Rome, 1956-1958), 2:252.

6– For an introduction to the literature concerning the Tupinambá, see Alfred Metraux, "The Tupinambá," *Handbook of South American Indians*, Julian H. Steward, ed. (Washington, D.C., 1948), 3: 95-13.

7– Marchant, *From Barter to Slavery*, chaps. 2-3.

8– On the donatarial period three articles by Paulo Merêa, Pedro Azevedo, and Carlos Malheiro Dias continue to be valuable, especially for the documents they reproduce. See Carlos Malheiro Dias, ed., *Historia da colonização portuguesa do Brasil*, 3 vols. (Porto, 1922-1924), 3:167-283.

9— Ruth Lapham Butler, "Thomé de Sousa, First Governor General of Brazil, 1549-1553," *Mid-America*, New Ser. (1942), 13:229-51, continues to be useful.

10— Brother Vicente Rodrigues to the Fathers and Brothers of Coimbra, Sept. 17, 1552, *MB*, 1:410.

11— In the preceding two paragraphs I have drawn rather freely from D. Alden, "The Early History of Bahía, 1501-1553" (M.S., M.A. thesis, University of California, Berkeley, 1952), chap. 7, where the discussion is based on coeval Jesuit letters.

12— Nóbrega to Padre Simão Rodrigues, Aug. 9, 1549, *MB*, 1:119-20.

13— Idem to idem, Jan. 6, 1550, *MB*, 1:166, where the text is given in Italian. I have followed the English translation that appears in John B. Stetson, Jr., trans. and ed., *The Histories of Brazil by Pero de Magalhães* [de Gandavo], 2 vols. (New York, 1922), 2:214-15, n. 44, where the precise date and the addressee of the document are missing.

14— Marchant, *From Barter to Slavery*, pp. 82f.

15— See Francisco Adolfo de Varnhagen, *História geral do Brasil antes da sua separação e independência de Portugal*, 5th ed. (São Paulo, 1956), 1:274-392, and 2:11-69, for details concerning expansion along the littoral during the second half of the sixteenth century.

16— Kiemen, pp. 4-5.

17— Kiemen, p. 4, states only that the law was adopted upon recommendation of the Mesa da Consciência e Ordens, a peninsular board charged with ecclesiastical affairs.

18— Stetson, 2:115-16.

19— For details, see *HCJB*, 2:155-69, 179, 617-22.

20— The text of the "Capítulos que Gabriel Soares de Sousa deu em Madrid ao Sr. D. Cristovam de Moura contra os padres da companhia de Jesus que residem no Brasil, com umas breves respostas dos mesmos padres. . ." was first published from a copy in Jesuit archives by Father Serafim Leite in *Ethnos, Revista do Instituto Português de Arquelogia, Historia e Etnografia* (Lisbon, 1941), 2:5-[36] and was reprinted (without such an indication) in *Anais da biblioteca nacional do Rio de Janeiro* (hereafter cited *ABNRJ*), 62:341-81. I am indebted to Professor Stuart Schwartz (University of Minnesota) for calling my attention to the *Ethnos* edition and for having provided me with a photographic copy of it.

21— *Tratado descriptivo do Brasil em 1587*, 2nd ed. (Rio de Janeiro, 1879), pp. 102-103, 111-12.

22— I am inclined to believe that José Honório Rodrigues dismisses much too lightly the significance of Sousa's "Charges" and the Jesuit responses they elicited. See his *Historiografia del Brasil. Siglo XVI* (Mexico, 1957), pp. 53-56.

23– It will be recalled that as a result of the failure of King Sebastian (1557-78) to provide an heir before his death, Philip II of Spain successfully laid claim to the vacant Portuguese throne, thereby initiating Portugal's so-called Babylonian Captivity (1580-1640).

24– Response to "Informção" no. 29.

25– For sources and further discussion concerning the legislation discussed in the two preceding paragraphs, see Kiemen, pp. 5-8.

26– It is significant that the presence of Indians is seldom mentioned in the detailed report on Brazil's eight northern captaincies (Porto Seguro to Rio Grande do Norte) prepared shortly after the turn of the seventeenth century. See Engel Sluiter, ed., "Report on the State of Brazil, 1612," *Hispanic American Historical Review* (1949), 29:518-62.

27– For a summary of the role of the bandeirantes in Brazilian history, see Affonso de E. Taunay, *História das bandeiras paulistas*, 2nd ed., 3 vols. (São Paulo, 1961), and for an introduction to the literature consult Richard M. Morse, comp., *The Bandeirantes; The Historical Role of the Brazilian Pathfinders* (New York, 1965).

28– I have attempted to summarize major scholarly findings concerning these raids in *Royal Government in Colonial Brazil* (Berkeley, 1968), chap. 3, pt. 2.

29– Charles R. Boxer, *Salvador de Sá and the Struggle for Brazil and Angola 1602-1686* (London, 1952), pp. 129-39 and 218.

30– Kiemen, p. 55.

31– For a brief sketch and references to the major biographies, see Charles R. Boxer, "A Great Luso-Brazilian Figure. Padre António Vieira, S. J., 1608-1697," *Diamante V* (London, 1957). I understand that Professor Boxer is now preparing a full-length biography of Vieira. It is much needed.

32– Vieira to John IV, May 20, 1653, João Lúcio de Azevedo, ed., *Cartas do Padre António Vieira* . . . , 3 vols. (Coimbra, 1925-28), 1:306-15.

33– Kiemen, pp. 84-85.

34– For his comprehensive proposals, see Vieira to John IV, Apr. 6, 1654, Azevedo, *Cartas*, 1:431-41; summarized in Kiemen, pp. 92-95, where the date given is in error.

35– Kiemen, pp. 98-99.

36– Vieira to John IV, Dec. 8, 1655, and Apr. 20, 1657, Azevedo, *Cartas*, 1:452-53, 467. The quotation is from the first letter.

37– Idem to idem, Apr. 20, 1657, p. 468.

38– Kiemen, pp. 104-16.

39– Provisão of Sept. 12, 1663, "Livro grosso do Maranhão," I, *ABNRJ* (1948), 66:31-32.

40– Kiemen, pp. 139-46.

41– João Lúcio de Azevedo, *Os Jesuitas no Grão-Pará* . . . (Lisbon, 1901), pp. 114-19.

43

42– *HCJB*, 4:87-92.

43– Pedro's dispatch of Dec. 31, 1686, to the General is quoted in ibid., pp. 91-92.

44– The full title was *Regimento das missões do estado do Maranhão e Grão Pará*.

45– The full text of the regimento, dated Dec. 21, 1686, is given in *HCJB*, 4:369-75; for a summary, see Kiemen, pp. 158-62.

46– Alvará of Apr. 28, 1688, *HCJB*, 4:377-80; summarized in Kiemen, pp. 164-66.

47– Kiemen, p. 163.

48– Three years earlier, in 1677, rumors circulated in the town of São Paulo that the governor of the neighboring captaincy of Rio de Janeiro intended to liberate all Indian slaves entering his territory. Fearful that such action would incite a general rebellion among the thousands of Indian slaves in São Paulo and convinced that the Black Robes must be behind such a threat, the Paulistas openly spoke of expelling the Jesuits from their college in São Paulo. After the Black Robes and the governor denied that there was any substance to the rumor, agitation subsided. Taunay, *Historia das bandeiras*, 1:123-24; *HCJB*, 6:306-307.

49– *HCJB*, 6:310-19.

50– According to Taunay, in 1691 "Estatuiu D. Pedro II que em caso algum poderiam os índios ser conservados em cativeiro." *Historia das bandeiras*, 1:126. He does not indicate where the text of such a law may be found and I have been unable to locate it in any of the usual sources.

51– *HCJB*, 6:318.

52– For a bio-bibliographical sketch of Lisbon-born Alexandre de Gusmão (1629-1724), who should not be confused with the later Santos-born figure who bore the same name and was the principal Portuguese architect of the Treaty of Madrid (1750), see *HCJB*, 8:289-98.

53– Gusmão, annual letter, May 30, 1694, *HCJB*, 6:323.

54– The original pact seems to have been dated about the middle of 1692. The only copy of its text that I have seen is in the annual letter of Father Gusmão of May 30, 1694, quoted in full in *HCJB*, 6:322-28.

55– Subsequent to the signing of the original agreement, two Franciscans (*Capuchos*) from Rio de Janeiro preached a Good Friday sermon in which they insisted that the Paulistas were the natural lords of the Indians and therefore had a right to obtain them in the back lands. The indignant king then insisted that the Paulistas sign the original agreement (in which they swore to desist from further slaving expeditions) once again. When upon order of the governor general the câmara complied, it affixed the "Doubts" described below in this paragraph. See the statement of Jan. 28, 1694, signed by the officers of the câmara and "moradores mais graves da terra," *Revista do Instituto Histórico e Geográfico Brasileiro* (hereafter cited as *RIHGB*), 3rd ed. (Rio de Janeiro, 1931), 7:370-74.

56— *RIHGB*, pp. 374-75; also published in *HCJB*, 6:328-30.

57— For bio-bibliographical details concerning Andreoni and Benci, see *HCJB*, 8.

58— According to António Vieira, none of the Jesuits favorable to the plan had experience among the Indians; at least, none could match his fourteen years as a missionary in Bahia and the Amazon. Vieira to Padre Manuel Luis, July 21, 1695, Azevedo, *Cartas*, 3:665-70.

59— By a dispatch of Jan. 14, 1693, cited in carta régia of Feb. 19, 1696, *RIHGB*, 7:282-86.

60— "Voto do Padre António Vieira sôbre as dúvidas dos moradores de S. Paulo acêrca da administração dos índios," July 12, 1694, *HCJB*, 6:330-41.

61— See Vieira to Duke of Cadaval, July 24, 1694, Azevedo, *Cartas*, 3:658.

62— See n. 59 above.

63— See Kiemen, pp. 7, 29, 31, 122, 141, 153-54, and 163. Lay captaincies had been authorized most recently in 1684 in Maranhão, but "became a dead letter" after the Beckman revolt. Kieman, p. 154. Curiously, six years before the king approved the Paulista plan, he ordered that no layman in the State of Brazil might become responsible for the management of Indian villages. Antonio Luis da Camara Coutinho (governor general) to Pedro II, June 19, 1691, reporting that none save ecclesiastics were serving in charge of *aldeias* within his State. Biblioteca Nacional, Rio de Janeiro, *Documentos historicos* (1936), 33:404.

64— I have reexamined some aspects of the Jesuits' expulsion in my "Economic Aspects of the Expulsion of the Jesuits from Brazil: A Preliminary Report," to be published in Henry H. Keith and S. Fred Edwards, eds., *Continuity and Conflict in Brazilian Society* (Columbia, S.C., in press).

65— One contemporary source that offers vivid testimony concerning the effects of the directorates upon the Indians of the Upper Amazon is Francisco Xavier Ribeiro de Sampaio, *Diario da viagem que em vista, e correição das povoações da capitania de S. José do Rio Negro, que fez o ouvidor, e intendente geral da mesma . . . no anno de 1774 e 1775* (Lisbon, 1825). For later appraisals, see Raiol (cited n. 1), pp. 147-62, and João Lúcio de Azevedo, *Estudos . . . paraense* (Pará, 1893), p. 149. Professor David M. Davidson (Cornell University) is preparing a study of the directorates based on his research in Brazilian and Portuguese archives. We badly need a scholarly study of the Paulista administrations. At least, I know of none.

66— *HCJB*, 6:312, 350-51.

67— This observation is based on a reading of the contemporary sources cited in this paper. As one example of the colonists' attitudes, see the early seventeenth-century *Diálogos das grandezas do Brasil* (cited n. 5), pp. 337, 340, 344-45; for the Jesuits' views, see the quotations in Boxer, *Race Relations*, pp. 88f.

68— *HCJB*, 6:346.

69— See especially Manuel da Nóbrega to Padre Miguel de Torres, May 8, 1558, *MB*, 2:447-59; also Boxer, *Race Relations*, pp. 90f.

Dutch Treatment of the American Indian, With Particular Reference to New Netherland

Allen W. Trelease

The Dutch overseas empire reached its peak in the 1650s. At that time it was, if not the largest, the most dynamic of the five European colonial systems, extending to India, Ceylon, Formosa, and the East Indies, western and southern Africa, Brazil, half a dozen islands in the Caribbean, and New Netherland on the Hudson and Delaware Rivers. When decline set in, two of the earliest and most important losses were American colonies, founded and maintained by the Dutch West India Company. Its control in Brazil lasted only twenty-four years (1630-54). New Netherland existed as a functioning colony only forty years before the English conquest of 1664 when the Dutch accepted Surinam or Dutch Guiana in return. Thus there was little time or territory within which to compile a massive colonial record in America. Moreover, time has taken a heavy toll of historical source material relating to Dutch America, most notably in the loss of the Dutch West India Company papers. The surviving record of Dutch-Indian relations is a spare one therefore, and in places it must remain conjectural.

Seventeenth-century Dutchmen, like the other colonizing peoples, assumed without question that European culture was richer, stronger, more highly developed, and closer to God than any other on earth. Certainly nothing they saw among the American

47

Indians did much to shake this conviction.[1] If clergymen and social reformers compared certain aspects of native life or practice favorably with conditions in their own society, it was to shame that society into living up to its own ideals. The minister at Ft. Orange (Albany), who repeated Mohawk criticisms of immorality among the local Dutch inhabitants, did not advocate abandoning the Dutch moral code and religious teachings but adhering to them. No one questioned that the Indians were a backward, ignorant, brutish, superstitious people who had infinitely more to learn from the Dutch than to teach them.[2]

Given the immense cultural gulf between them, it is not surprising that Indians and white men made little effort or progress toward assimilation in the seventeenth century. The Indians were generally unwilling to adopt most of the white man's ways until their own civilization had become eroded through sustained contact. The Dutch, for their part, did less than most powers to bridge the gap. Even more than the British, they appear to have followed a policy of live and let live so far as acculturation, assimilation, and religious conversion were concerned. The most important reason for this neglect was the secularity of Dutch life at home, which was more highly commercialized and cosmopolitan than anywhere else in Europe. Political and religious toleration were farther advanced than in England and bore no comparison to the tight Catholic orthodoxy of Spain, Portugal, and even France. Both at home and abroad the Dutch found it less possible and less congenial to force conformity on religious, political, and racial minorities.

In Dutch America, the cultural, religious, and racial barriers which were felt to exist between Indians and whites created a kind of de facto segregation or apartheid rather than persecution, proscription, or forced conversion. Miscegenation between Dutch and Indians was fairly rare and intermarriage was almost unknown. In New Netherland there were enough Dutch or other European women to go around, and in colonies like Brazil or the East Indies where there were not, male colonists tended to marry Portuguese Creole girls. The latter may well have had Indian or Negro blood, for the Portuguese, like the Spanish and French, intermixed more with native peoples everywhere.[3] Race prejudice doubtless played a part in this Dutch attitude, but in their own eyes the basic difference between themselves and the Indians was religious. This was the ground for an early enactment against miscegenation with the Indians around Ft. Orange.[4] The few children of such liaisons appear to have been accepted into the Dutch community provided they were brought up in the Dutch church and Dutch ways. Religion was also the key to intermarriage and assimilation in the Dutch Asiatic colonies where it occurred much more frequently. If the Indians had desired integration into the Dutch community, race prejudice might well have hampered or prevented it, but so few became Christian converts that the question of race prejudice per se seldom arose. As it was, most of the overt race prejudice was reserved for the Negroes who were held as slaves in nearly every Dutch colony.[5]

The missionary impulse was not altogether lacking among the Dutch. Conversion of the Indians to Christianity was always sought in theory, and it was commonly regarded as a prerequisite to (or accompaniment of) a more general civilizing mission. But the few Dutch ministers in America who seriously tried to work among the Indians labored under certain disadvantages which the clergy of other powers did not fully share. Some of these handicaps lay in the character of the Dutch Reformed Church as opposed to the Roman Catholicism of the French, Spanish, and Portuguese. Catholicism, with its ritual, ceremony, and visible symbols of faith, had a naturally greater appeal to a people whose own religion and ways of thought were expressed in a symbolism drawn from the physical world and their forest environment. How many Indians penetrated beyond Catholicism's outer symbolism is another matter, but very few were ready to appreciate the introspective and unadorned Calvinism offered them by the Dutch Reformed Church. Moreover, the Protestant churches, including the Dutch Reformed, had more demanding requirements for baptism and nominal conversion. French Jesuits among the Iroquois, for instance, baptized almost any Indian who requested it—and many who did not—with little regard for age or previous instruction. Although their full acceptance into the church was still to come, such persons were often claimed as converts. Dutch missionaries, on the other hand, were permitted to confer baptism only on adult Indians (or their children) who had demonstrated a genuine conversion to the faith based on prior education and understanding. In other words, some acculturation was required in the first place, and very few Indians attained it until their own culture had largely disintegrated.[6] This stage had barely begun in parts of New Netherland when the colony passed out of Dutch hands; Dutch control in Brazil was even shorter.

A further advantage of the Catholic powers in winning converts lay in the fact that they had preceded the Dutch in nearly every colony. This was true of the Portuguese in Brazil, the Spanish in the West Indies, and, to a degree, the French among the Iroquois. When the Dutch won control in these areas, most of the Indians who were amenable to conversion were already at least nominal Catholics. The Dutch made little or no effort to win them over to the Reformed religion and often allowed Catholic missionaries to continue their work.

In the Dutch West Indies very few natives survived the earlier Spanish occupation. Most of those who did come into contact with the Dutch lived on the island of Aruba, where they retained their nominal Catholic faith without hindrance. By the early nineteenth century they had intermarried so extensively with the newer African population and with the very few Dutch colonists that each element lost its individuality and merged into what a historian of the island calls the Aruban race.[7] On the other Dutch islands (Curaçao, Bonaire, St. Martin, St. Eustatius, and Saba), the Indians had either vanished by the time the Dutch arrived in the early seventeenth century, or they were so few in number that they disappeared much sooner through removal or assimilation, leaving little trace behind.

The Indians in Surinam or Dutch Guiana occupied a large jungle hinterland which the Dutch have not effectively penetrated to this day. Two or three thousand Indians still live in parts of this territory with little change in their condition over three hundred years. Very little assimilation has taken place because the Indians, after destructive warfare with the early colonists, withdrew into the bush to avoid it, and the Dutch have made little effort to pursue them. For a long time these Indians have been outnumbered, even in their own element, by Negro bushmen, the descendants of escaped African slaves, who are hardly more acculturated themselves.[8]

The Brazilian Indians, too, remained largely apart from the Dutch and from the Portuguese who preceded and followed the Dutch. As on Aruba, most of the Indians who adopted Christianity were Catholic converts won over by the Portuguese. The Dutch did make a few native converts, however, and sent some of their children to the Netherlands for schooling. Some of these relapsed into savagery when they returned to Brazil, while others virtually abandoned their original culture and language and became completely Europeanized.[9]

So far as New Netherland is concerned, only two ministers made any serious effort to work with the Indians, and they almost certainly failed to make a single convert. The one boy whom they trained to read Dutch and participate in divine service backslid into drunkenness and did more harm than good among his people, they reported.[10]

For the most part the Dutch and Indians lived apart physically as well as culturally. They treated each other as separate powers, equal in theory and sometimes in practice. The Dutch came to America for trade and empire; in seeking these they dealt with the Indians primarily as possessors of land to be acquired, as sources of trade and wealth, and as political and military powers who were to be negotiated with, fought as enemies, or courted as allies. The expansion and prosperity—even the very existence of some of the colonies—demanded that these matters be given priority as long as the Indians clung to their independence and retained their freedom of action.

Acquisition of the Indians' land was perhaps the most fundamental part of Indian relations in New Netherland, as in all colonies where Europeans settled in significant numbers. Both the Dutch and Indians in this region were agrarians, and for each the possession and use of the land were fundamental conditions of life. Dutch policy and practice in this regard was liberal. From the beginning they recognized the Indians' prior ownership and hence the legal necessity, as well as expediency, of buying land before appropriating it. In

1652 it was further provided that no land could be purchased from the Indians without prior governmental approval. In the short run the natives likely gained more than they lost by this measure. Although it probably hastened their displacement by eliminating speculators, lowering land prices, and facilitating white settlement, it also removed some of the opportunity for fraud and high-pressure tactics by individuals dealing with the tribesmen for their own advantage. Doubtless the Indians were still defrauded in some land transactions and subjected to undue pressure in others, but this was the exception rather than the rule. The prices they received were generally satisfactory at the time of the sales, and although these figures appear ridiculously low today—as the legendary $24 for Manhattan Island—present real estate values did not apply three hundred years ago, either for buyer or seller. Furthermore, much of the land which the Dutch bought around New Amsterdam was purchased so far ahead of actual need that the Indians continued to occupy it undisturbed for years after the purchase.[11]

Nevertheless the Dutch were constantly plagued by land disputes with the neighboring Indians. These quarrels proceeded much less from dishonesty or sharp practice on either side than from different concepts of land tenure and alienation. For the Indians, land was a community resource which belonged to the tribe or band as a whole for the use of its members in perpetuity; it was not a commodity to be bought or sold. Many transactions which the Dutch looked upon as final sales were apparently regarded by the natives as payments for temporary use, subject to later cancellation and retrocession. As land prices rose with more intensive settlement, the Indians sometimes assumed that they had been defrauded in selling earlier at a lower price. For these reasons they sometimes demanded further payment or asked the white occupants to leave. The Dutch were not fully aware of the reasons for these demands and reacted variously according to the troublemaking capacity of the natives involved. Sometimes they refused repayment, but more often they complied, as the money involved was less than the cost of coping with continuing discontent, depredations, or even war. Staten Island was purchased three times—twice by the Dutch and once by the English—before the Indians finally surrendered their claims. In nearly every case these disputes were settled peacefully, but by 1659 mutual depredations by Dutch settlers and the Esopus Indians, near modern Kingston, New York, erupted into a war which lasted intermittently for five years. The Indians lost and ended up ceding far more land than the original tract in dispute.[12]

In the West Indies and South American colonies, Indian title seems generally to have passed away in the areas of Dutch settlement before they took over, and land purchase was apparently of less importance. Although Dutch land policy was liberal by the standards of other powers and was carried out with relative fairness, the neighboring tribes still lost their lands in the long run. Given the fact of colonization, no other result was likely or even possible.

The second major concern of Dutch-Indian relations in New Netherland was the fur trade. This was the economic base upon which the colony had been founded, and long after farmers had come to outnumber traders, it remained the major source of revenue. In this commerce, unlike almost every other economic activity, the two races were interdependent—each was essential to the other's prosperity. For several reasons Dutch traders never ventured into the interior for furs, like the Canadian *coureurs de bois*. Instead the natives, who trapped all the animals themselves, brought the furs to the settlements to exchange for a variety of European trading goods. At first the trade was fairly widespread, but within a few years the seaboard fur supply became exhausted and activity centered at Ft. Orange and near the later site of Philadelphia, close to the heads of navigation on the Hudson and Delaware Rivers, respectively. The most prominent suppliers of peltry were the powerful Iroquois tribes of New York and the Susquehanna of Pennsylvania. A good relationship with these inland tribes was essential to both the prosperity and safety of New Netherland.

Dutch fur traders, like those of other nations, were not noted for refinement of taste or manners. Many of them were repeatedly guilty of cheating the Indians and each other, of hiring brokers or high-pressure salesmen to intercept the natives on their way into the settlements with furs, of enticing Indians into their houses, and even of forcibly kidnapping them to get their peltry. Trade regulations were enacted to prevent these abuses, but enforcement was difficult and they continued through the years. On the other hand, Iroquois hunters caused a high casualty rate among the settlers' livestock. But the friction engendered by these practices never led to war or even a serious war scare. The trade was too profitable to both sides.

Land disputes seldom arose with these tribes, for they usually lived at a distance from the white settlements. When the Indians demanded guns and ammunition in return for their furs, the Dutch supplied them in such quantity that these tribes, and particularly the Iroquois, became the strongest Indian powers on that part of the continent. Because of this power, the Dutch in turn courted their support against aggressive New Englanders and hostile Indians farther south. This relationship developed into a full-fledged political and military alliance after the English conquest of 1664, but the English built on a foundation laid by the Dutch.[13]

A comparable relationship existed between the Dutch of Brazil and the warlike and cannibalistic Tapuya tribes of the interior. Trade was less a factor here than the Indians' military power and their hostility to the Portuguese. The Dutch deliberately courted these tribes, and, without their support, the Portuguese would surely have recaptured the colony sooner than they did. By contrast the Dutch enjoyed a lesser rapport with the coastal Tupis who had come under the influence of the Portuguese earlier and had remained somewhat within their orbit.[14]

Indian relations along the lower Hudson and around New Amsterdam also took a different course from those at Ft. Orange, passing through three rather distinct phases. There was an initial period of fifteen or twenty years in which relations were generally placid; the white population was small, widely scattered, and much involved in the fur trade. Land disputes seldom arose and the local Algonquian tribesmen were valuable as suppliers of peltry. A second phase of about twenty years, beginning around 1640, was characterized by the rapid increase of white population, expanding the periphery of settlement; trade and dependence upon the Indians declined, their lands came to be in high demand, and each side came progressively to regard the other as a menace. These tribes were not supplied with guns as were those farther north, and this fact in itself became a grievance to the Indians. Multiplying frictions culminated in intermittent warfare which the Indians generally lost. The final stage found the Indians defeated, and gradually they left, died off, or remained behind in a condition of increasing demoralization and dependence on the white man.

During the intermediate period of stress the Dutch followed two consecutive policies. Governor Willem Kieft's approach in the 1640s was to intimidate the Indians and, failing that, to exterminate them. In 1643 he precipitated a war by an unprovoked attack on two parties of Indians near New Amsterdam. About eleven bands of natives in northern New Jersey, Long Island, and the lower Hudson took the warpath in retaliation, wiping out nearly every Dutch settlement outside New Amsterdam. For a time the town itself was under such close siege that no one could go out for a stick of firewood without a military escort. The Dutch prevailed after two years of fighting, but at tremendous cost to the colony.[15]

Governor Kieft was recalled to Holland in disgrace, and his successor, Peter Stuyvesant, adopted a policy of appeasement which fully satisfied neither side. He repurchased lands which had been under cultivation for years, he denied armaments to trigger-happy colonists while supplying them sparingly to insistent tribesmen, he did what he could to punish individual cases of mistreating Indians, and he tried vainly to stem the demoralizing flow of liquor to them. But none of this brought lasting peace. The Indians made an armed incursion into New Amsterdam in 1655 which came very close to precipitating another war. In 1659 the land difficulties at the Esopus, halfway up the Hudson, did lead to a war which the Dutch ultimately won in 1664.[16]

This victory finally established a firm peace on the lower Hudson, but it occurred only four months before New Netherland itself succumbed to English conquest. New York fought no wars with the neighboring Indians because the Dutch had already established European supremacy, and there was no longer a will or capacity to resist among these Algonquian tribesmen. If events followed a happier course elsewhere—on the upper Hudson and in Brazil—it was because white settlement did not reach the stage at which the Indians felt engulfed. The two peoples were still free to pursue coexistence at arm's length.

Most Indians lived at such a distance that they formed no real part of Dutch colonial society and seldom if ever came within the purview of Dutch law. The few who did were clearly regarded and treated as second-class citizens. They were frequently exploited or taken advantage of economically, but this was limited in some degree by legal safeguards—only the Negro lacked any rights at all which the white man was bound to respect. Indian slavery was unknown in New Netherland, save for a few prisoners of war who were sent out of the colony. In Brazil Indians were kidnapped and enslaved contrary to the West India Company's categorical orders, but this practice was unusual. In Surinam the same practice led to such bitter Indian warfare that it was suppressed by the colonial government.[17]

The earliest regulations governing the colonists of New Netherland required them "faithfully to fulfill their promises to the Indians . . . and not to give them any offense without cause as regards their persons, wives, or property," and the natives were always to be shown "honesty, faithfulness, and sincerity," so as to avoid any cause of hostility. Moreover, Dutchmen committing offenses against Indians were to be speedily punished. To set such a policy is not automatically to practice it, but the intention was clear. Recognition of the Indians' prior landownership has already been mentioned together with the general willingness to settle land disputes to their satisfaction. Governor Stuyvesant, in particular, intervened personally to settle some of the more serious cases, and his inclination was usually to give the Indians the benefit of any doubts. In addition there were protective measures such as the rules governing conduct of the fur trade and a law of 1640 forbidding colonists to let their livestock stray into Indians' unfenced cornfields. The courts, on occasion, punished colonists for infractions of these rules as well as for cheating or otherwise mistreating Indians.[18]

Throughout the history of New Netherland there was a host of enactments aimed at stopping the liquor traffic with Indians.

They had had no experience with intoxicants before the Europeans' arrival and avidly made up for the deprivation afterward. They were willing to pay a high price for Dutch beer and brandy, and there were plenty of colonists willing to supply the demand without much regard for the consequences. The tribesmen lacked the psychological and social controls to keep drinking within bounds, and while drunk some of them ran amuck, committing indiscriminate mayhem against each other and the whites. Liquor threatened to demoralize tribal society, and Indian sachems were therefore among the earliest prohibitionists in America. The liquor traffic was also open to various abuses by the Dutch suppliers—such as overcharging and watering down the beverage—which caused Indian resentment when it was discovered. Although Indian testimony was not ordinarily received in court, it came to be accepted in cases of liquor-law infractions at least.[19] The efforts to prevent this traffic were well meaning, but they failed as abysmally then as in the 1920s, for the profits were high and a great part of the community was implicated.

As the preambles to many ordinances make clear, the authorities in Holland and America were motivated in protecting Indian rights as much by a desire to avoid their wrath and retaliation as to serve the ends of abstract justice. Their very weakness at times led the Dutch to follow a course of appeasement when they would otherwise have taken a higher hand. Moreover, their smaller numbers, compared with other colonial peoples, did less to threaten the Indians with displacement, hence did less to awaken their hostility. Wherever Dutch colonists settled around the world, they left a strong impression that the peaceful and law-abiding elements of the Netherlands population had stayed at home. As they were given to brawling, boisterousness, and sharp practice among themselves, it is no wonder that Indians sometimes received like treatment. But at the same time they were more cosmopolitan and more tolerant of cultural diversity and nonconformity than any other colonial people. Spanish and Portuguese observers admitted that the Dutch treated the Indians with greater kindliness and tact than they, and won greater native support as a result.[20] If they did less to prepare the Indians for ultimate assimilation, that was agreeable to the Indians themselves.

These distinctions, however, are ones of emphasis and circumstance. Viewed in perspective, Dutch treatment of the Indians resembles much more than it differs from that of their European contemporaries. Wherever Europeans settled in numbers, Indian society was drastically modified, if not altogether destroyed.

NOTES

1— For a discussion of Dutch racial attitudes and mixing with native peoples, especially in Asia, see Charles R. Boxer, *The Dutch Seaborne Empire, 1600-1800* (New York, 1965), chap. 8.

2— See, for example, J. F. Jameson, ed., *Narratives of New Netherland, 1609-1664* (New York, 1909), pp. 126-29.

3— Boxer, *Dutch Seaborne Empire*, pp. 227-29.

4— A. J. F. Van Laer, ed., *Van Rensselaer Bowier Manuscripts* (Albany, 1908), p. 442.

5— Allen W. Trelease, *Indian Affairs in Colonial New York: The Seventeenth Century* (Ithaca, N.Y., 1960), p. 172; Boxer, *Dutch Seaborne Empire*, pp. 215-41.

6— Trelease, *Indian Affairs*, pp. 38-40, 169-72.

7— Johan Hartog, *Aruba Past and Present*, J. A. Verleun, trans. (Oranjestad, Aruba, c. 1961), pp. 28-29, 45-46, 77, 111, 217.

8— Philip Hanson Hiss, *Netherlands America: The Dutch Territories in the West* (New York, c. 1943), pp. 71-74, 190.

9— Charles R. Boxer, *The Dutch in Brazil, 1624-1654* (Oxford, 1957), pp. 134-37.

10— Edmund B. O'Callaghan, ed., *Documentary History of the State of New-York*, octavo ed., 4 vols. (Albany, 1849-51), 3: 108; Trelease, *Indian Affairs*, pp. 169-71.

11— Trelease, *Indian Affairs*, pp. 36, 40-41, 43-45, 62-64, 91-93.

12— Ibid., pp. 11-12, 62-63, 91-93, 150-51, 159, 168, 195.

13— Ibid., chap. 5.

14— Boxer, *Dutch in Brazil*, pp. 52, 134-36, 185, and *passim*.

15— Trelease, *Indian Affairs*, chap. 3.

16— Ibid., chaps. 4, 6.

17— Ibid., pp. 81, 158-60; Boxer, *Dutch in Brazil*, p. 137.

18— A. J. F. Van Laer, ed., *Documents Relating to New Netherland, 1624-1626, in the Henry E. Huntington Library* (San Marino, Calif., 1924), docs. A, C, D, and E; Trelease, *Indian Affairs*, pp. 37-38, 64-65, 159-60.

19— Trelease, *Indian Affairs*, pp. 70, 93-94, 125-26, 135, 168-69.

20— Boxer, *Dutch in Brazil*, pp. 136-37.

The French and the Indians

Mason Wade

Despite all the work that has been done upon this subject by many French Canadian and some American scholars since 1867, when Francis Parkman's *The Jesuits in North America* first appeared, I still have to concur with his verdict that while "Spanish civilization crushed the Indian; English civilization scorned and neglected him; French civilization embraced and cherished him."[1] I have made no special study of Spanish behavior towards the aborigines, but I have done enough work on American colonial history to realize the truth of Joseph Choate's remark made in an address to the Pilgrim Society: "The first thing that our forefathers did when they landed on these shores was to fall upon their knees and thank God; the second was to fall upon the Indian." The French record is less genocidal and considerably more inspiring.

That record is perhaps familiar but some of its high points must be reviewed as the basis of any critical judgment. The record begins with Jacques Cartier's kidnapping of two Iroquoian Indians, who were fishing in the Bay of Chaleur in the summer of 1534, when Cartier raised a great cross at Gaspé bearing the fleur-de-lis and the inscription *Vive le roi de France!*[2]—a fitting symbol of the close future relationship between church and state in the New France thus claimed. It was the tall tales told by these Indians of the rich mythi-

61

cal kingdoms of Hochelaga, Stadacona, and the Saguenay—which might be new Mexicos, Perus, or the outposts of Cathay itself—that aroused French interest in the New World. They induced a greedy François I to back Cartier's voyages in the following year, when the latter made his way up the St. Lawrence to the Mohawk settlement of Stadacona (Quebec) and the Huron or Onondaga town of Hochelaga (Montreal), and again in 1541-42, when colonization for the first time was Cartier's aim, in order to establish a base for further search for the Northwest Passage and the discovery of the riches of the mythical kingdom of the Saguenay.

The strong missionary impulse of the Catholic revival or Counter Reformation in France is evident in the opening dedication to His Most Christian Majesty in Cartier's *Brief Récit*, the account of his second voyage, in which the navigator of St. Malo holds forth "the certain hope of the future augmentation of our said Holy Faith and of your seigneuries and Most Christian Name." Cartier had been taken for a god by the Indians of Hochelaga, to whom he read the Gospel of St. John and gave gifts, after they had besought him to touch the sores of their sick, "as if God had come there to cure them." With a foreshadowing of that friendly relationship with the Indians which was to be the great buckler of New France in its long struggle against the English, Cartier observed: "By what we have seen and been able to understand of these people it seems to me that they should be easy to tame. May God in His holy compassion see to it. Amen."[3] To achieve his high-minded ends, Cartier did not hesitate to kidnap Chief Donnacona, his two sons, and eight of his band, taking them back to France in the spring of 1536.

It was not until 1540—the same year in which the Society of Jesus was founded—that conversion of the savages became an official goal of French enterprise in the New World. François I intended to create a permanent French colony among the savages "in order to attain better our announced intention and to do something pleasing to God our creator and redeemer and which may lead to the augmentation of His holy and sacred name and of our mother Holy Catholic Church of whom we are called and named the first son."[4] But Donnacona and the other Indians all died in France, after being duly baptized, before Cartier returned to the St. Lawrence in 1541, although the Indian chief had told the French king of "many mines of gold and silver in great abundance"[5] in the Kingdom of Saguenay. The list of men required for Cartier's third voyage concluded with six churchmen, who seemingly had a far lower priority than "two goldsmiths and lapidaries,"[6] although the ostensible purpose of the expedition was "to establish the Christian Religion in a country of savages separated from France by all the extent of the earth, and where he [the King] knew that there were no mines of gold and silver, nor other gain to be hoped for than the conquest of infinite souls for God, and their deliverance from the domination and tyranny of the infernal Demon, to whom they sacrificed even their own children." This missionary motive, so often assigned to the early French discoverers by French Canadian clerical writers, was probably mere pious lip service, a convention of a highly religious period, masking a very modern interest in acquiring wealth.

There is no mention of missionary work being begun during Cartier's third voyage, but an enthusiastic record of the discovery at Cape Rouge of a "good store of stones, which we esteemed to be diamants," "a goodly Myne of the best iron in the world," "certaine leaves of fine gold as thick as a man's nayle," "veines of mynerall matter, which shewe like gold and silver," and "stones like Diamants, the most faire, pollished and excellently cut that it is possible for a man to see, when the Sunne shineth upon them, they glister as it were sparkles of fire." So, after planting a garden and an acre and a half of turnips and beginning the construction of a fort at Cap Rouge, Cartier soon set off to Hochelaga, "of purpose to view and understand the fashion of the Sault of water, which are to be passed to goe to Saguenay, that hee might be the readier in the spring to passe farther."[7] The search for the riches of the kingdom of the Saguenay was more pressing than laying a firm base in colonization and missionary activity.

It is interesting to note that on this trip, during which Cartier examined the St. Mary's and Lachine Rapids and learned of the Long Sault on the Ottawa, he left two young French boys with the Indians to learn their language in exchange for the two Indian children entrusted to him in 1536. This early exchange scholarship plan, later continued by Champlain, was to serve New France well. For the French had the good fortune, unlike other European newcomers, to find themselves among the largest linguistic family of the North American Indians, and the expertise their interpreters soon acquired in the Algonkian and Huronian tongues spoken in the St. Lawrence-Great Lakes region stood them in good stead in the incredibly rapid expansion of the fur trade to the foothills of the Rockies, the western limit of the Algonkian linguistic family, and in their later dealings with the Iroquois. The commercial necessity of acquiring the Indian tongues for purposes of trade was furthered by the missionary motive, for, as the Jesuit Father Paul Lejeune later recognized at the outset of his missions in 1632 and 1633, "anyone who knew their language perfectly would be powerful among them," and "How could a mute preach the Gospel?"[8] He realized that his first tasks were to learn Montagnais and to compile a dictionary, for which there was no precedent except for Father Brébeuf's effort of 1625. The lot of the student of colonial history would be far easier if Frenchman and Englishman had heard the same sounds in the same fashion, but each had his own system of transliteration, and the French and English variations on the same Indian words are so great as to suggest that the linguistic phenomena of the "Anglo-Saxon Tin Ear" and "magnificent unilingualism" were highly developed even in early days.

Later in the French regime, when conquest by religion had failed, the French attitude toward the Indians became more like the English one. When Cadillac founded Detroit in 1703 he called for priests to teach the savages French, which he thought would civilize them more surely than Christianity. Eventually the missionaries could evangelize, but the Indians should first become "subjects of the king, and afterwards . . . Christians."[9] The "Apostle of the Indians," John Eliot of Massachusetts, was virtually unique among seventeenth-century New Englanders in his concern about learning the Indian tongues and preaching to them in their own language. The early English New Yorkers had to rely upon Dutch interpreters in their Indian negotiations. Sir William Johnson was the first British officer to acquire the command of Indian speech and the firsthand familiarity with Indian life that had long been commonplace among the Canadian military leaders and were to prove so helpful in mustering and leading savage allies to offset the heavy odds against the vastly outnumbered French in the great struggle for empire in North America.

After Cartier, French interest in the New World languished for half a century. Then, in 1589, François Du Pont-Gravé, a St. Malo merchant, and Pierre Chauvin, a Huguenot captain of Honfleur, both of whom were active in the fur trade, obtained a ten-year monopoly on Canadian trade. In 1600 they set up a trading post at Tadoussac at the mouth of the Saguenay River, long a rendezvous of the Indians, French fishermen, and Basque whalers. The post failed to flourish, and the monopoly was annulled in 1602 and given to the Company of New France, a joint-stock company with a royal charter on the same model as the English and Dutch companies trading with the East Indies. Its field of activity was defined as from Florida to the Arctic Circle and westward as far as the forces of the rivers flowing into the St. Lawrence or the "Fresh Sea" (Great Lakes). It had a complete monopoly of commerce for only fifteen years, but it monopolized the fur trade forever. In return the company promised to settle four thousand colonists in New France within fifteen years, maintaining them for the first three years and thereafter assisting them. It was to see to the conversion of the natives and the preservation of Catholicism among orthodox French colonists, who were to be the only ones tolerated. Perhaps the chief merit of the company was its monopoly which helped to keep rival traders from debauching their Indian suppliers in competitive trade.

In the charters of this and subsequent French companies founded during the seventeenth century there was an emphasis on the "reputation of the Crown" as well as on the "glory of God," which reflected the rivalry of the new nation states and the missionary instincts of the Counter Reformation. The companies were a means for a poor monarchy to build an empire at the expense of the merchant stockholders. But while the companies met with varying commercial success in the fur trade's typical cycle of poverty and

plenty, they failed miserably as colonization agents and only tolerated the missionary activity which they were supposed to support.
None of the successive French companies fulfilled its promises of
colonization, and it was only after the influential Society of Jesus
secured private support from great nobles of the French court that
missionary work was begun on any serious scale.

The first Company of New France sent out its initial expedition in 1603 under the command of Du Pont-Gravé, who was accompanied by Samuel de Champlain, a Catholic who impartially had
fought under the Protestant Henry of Navarre in the Wars of the
League and served in the Spanish forces in the West Indies. Henry IV
had commissioned his old comrade in arms as a royal geographer in
reward for Champlain's published account of New Spain. It was in
this capacity that Champlain accompanied Du Pont-Gravé in 1603,
for this was an exploring expedition, seeking a suitable site for settlement as well as engaging in trade.

At Tadoussac in 1603 an alliance was made with the Montagnais which lasted as long as New France did. The French, unlike
the Spaniards and the English, did not try to exterminate the relatively sparse Indian population in their region of exploration because they needed their aid in the fur trade and in war against their
more numerous white rivals. Circumstances forced them into an alliance with the Algonkian tribes of eastern North America (the Montagnais of the lower St. Lawrence, the Micmacs, Etchemins, Abena-
kis of Acadia and Maine, and the Algonquins of the Ottawa Valley—
who were already the middlemen in the trade of furs for French
goods) against the Iroquois confederacy, who had been driven back
by 1603 from the St. Lawrence Valley to their eventual homeland in
northern New York. The sides were unconsciously being chosen for
the great battle between rival empires in North America, for the Iroquois, after nearly nipping French colonization in the bud on their
own, were to become the allies of the English in the struggle for military dominance and control of the fur trade in the interior. The Iroquois were to be the most dreaded enemies of the French, but the
hands of all other Indians of northeastern America were raised
against the Iroquois because of their ferocious love of war, and so the

French won the alliance of the greater part of the Indians in the region they were to penetrate. Without these Indian allies, chronically undermanned New France could not have survived as long as it did.

From the first the French proved willing to learn from the Indians. Champlain's experience with the Richelieu rapids, and later with the St. Mary's and Lachine Rapids at Montreal, convinced him that the Indian canoe, "which a man can easily carry," must be adopted instead of the clumsy French skiff if the French were to explore the country. He also became convinced that "by directing one's course with the help of the savages and their canoes, a man may see all that is to be seen, good and bad, within the space of a year or two."[10] This prompt French recognition of the superiority of the light birch bark Indian canoe was as epoch making as the introduction of European tools, utensils, and weapons into North America. With the aid of the canoe, the French were able to explore the waterways of the continent during the next century and trace out the routes which were later used by Frenchmen who had mastered, as well as any Indian, the use of the canoe for trade, exploration, and warfare. The willingness of the French to adapt themselves to native ways gave them a great advantage over the insular English, who long thought the English way was the only way. The Hudson's Bay Company did not adopt the canoe for nearly a century after it began operations.

Having acquired a fair idea of the St. Lawrence-Great Lakes system in a single summer, in the next three years, 1604-1607, Champlain explored and mapped the Atlantic coast from Nova Scotia to the juncture of Martha's Vineyard and Nantucket Sounds. Brushes with hostile Indians along the densely populated Massachusetts coast led Poutrincourt to return to Port Royal and its friendly Micmacs, although Champlain wished to explore farther southward. Unfriendly Indians thus prevented the French from finding a site for settlement on Narragansett Bay, the Connecticut shore, or New York harbor; French colonization struggled against harsher conditions in the colder and less fertile regions to the north. At Port Royal the French and Indians helped provision one another, and Membertou and other Indian chiefs were welcomed to the Frenchmen's table at the Habitation with a lack of racial feeling which was to be one of the great assets of the French in North America. Young Biencourt and Du Pont-Gravé adapted themselves to Indian ways and learned Micmac, and Champlain determined to settle other young Frenchmen among the Indians to become agents and interpreters. The French supplied their Indian friends with muskets and steel-tipped arrows which enabled Membertou to conduct a successful war party against the fierce Armouchiquois of Norumbega, whom the English later called the Massachusetts. Fishhooks, kettles, other ironware, ornaments, and European clothing also were adopted by the Indians, who in return taught the French the use of tobacco, many tricks of forest craft, and canoeing. Though the French planted gardens at Saint-Croix and Port Royal, the Micmacs were not agricultural Indians and could not be induced to follow suit. When moose meat, their staple food, was not available, they had to be saved from starving by French provisions. They acquired an unbridled taste for brandy as well as wine and soon complained that "since the French mingle with and carry on trade with them, they are dying fast and the population is thinning out."[11] They thought the French poisoned them, but Father Biard rightly blamed their own gluttony and drunkenness.

The revocation of De Monts' trading monopoly in 1607, and the destruction of Port Royal and the Jesuit settlement of St. Sauveur on the Maine coast in 1613 by Samuel Argall of Virginia, virtually wiped out the French effort at colonization in Acadia. The tide of settlement shifted to Quebec, which Champlain founded in 1608. While he laid the basis of good French relations with the Indians, it was first the Recollet and later the Jesuit missionaries who developed these relations into a close and lasting alliance. One of the reasons for choosing Quebec as a base was that it would be "easier to plant the Christian faith and establish such order as is necessary for the protection of a country"[12] among the sedentary Indians of the interior. The new settlement would discourage raids by the Iroquois on the fur traffic and enable the French to meet the Indians at the Lachine Rapids, a natural entrepôt at the crossroads of three great waterways. Champlain's desire to explore further met opposition from the Montagnais who did not wish to lose the profitable role of middlemen in the exchange of northern furs for French goods. The French were to meet similar opposition from other adjacent tribes as they pressed westward. But the Indians were only too willing to have French aid in their war parties against the Iroquois, and Champlain's participation in that of 1609 by the Montagnais, Algonquins, and Hurons had momentous consequences for the French in North America.

The Iroquois were encountered on Lake Champlain near the future site of Fort Ticonderoga, and Champlain's double-loaded harquebus, which killed two of their three chiefs at the first shot, was sufficient to put the much stronger Iroquois party to panic-stricken flight. This exploit sealed the alliance of the French with the Algonkians and the Hurons and fixed their deadly enmity with the Iroquois. Thanks to this war party, it was a long time before the French found their way up the St. Lawrence beyond the Lachine Rapids, which were barred by the Iroquois. Like the Hurons, they were forced to follow the arduous Ottawa River route. Actually they had had little choice in the matter for the St. Lawrence would still have been barred to them unless they had allied themselves with the Iroquois. This alliance was impossible since the French fur trade and the future of the French establishments on the St. Lawrence hinged upon the friendship of the Algonkians and the Hurons.

In June of 1610 Champlain also founded the long line of French *coureurs de bois* by persuading the Algonquins to take home with them a young Frenchman, Etienne Brûlé, while the French agreed to take a young Huron, Savignon, to France. These "exchange students" were to be returned the following May. Thus Brûlé became the first of the later numerous Frenchmen who lived with the Indians and gave their compatriots great advantages by their knowledge of Indian languages and customs. In 1611 Champlain arranged to have another Frenchman winter with the Hurons to learn their language, as Brûlé already had that of the Algonquins, while Savignon returned home with the Hurons to spread the prestige of the French among them. Champlain also arranged with Tessouat, an Algonquin chief whom he had met at Tadoussac in 1603, to take home another young Frenchman, Nicolas de Vignau. Henceforth these three young Frenchmen could serve him as guides and interpreters. By proposing to found an establishment at Montreal, Champlain tightened his ties with the Hurons and Algonquins, since they would be saved the long and dangerous journey to Tadoussac or Quebec. The way was open for future exploration through their territory.

Champlain had higher motives than most of the French fur traders, as his efforts in France to secure missionaries indicate. He may have held some resentment against the Jesuits for their decision in 1610 to go to Acadia instead of to Quebec as he had asked. In any case the order, with its Spanish connections, was not popular either with the Prince de Condé, the absentee governor of New France, or with the northern Huguenot merchants. So Champlain sought instead "some good friars, with zeal and affection for the glory of God, whom I might persuade to send or come themselves with me to this country to plant there the faith."[13] He found them among the Recollets of Brouage—the Recollets were an ascetic branch of the Franciscans—who volunteered to a man for the Canadian mission. But they were a poor order and had no funds to maintain missionaries. Funds were secured from the French bishops, who had assembled for a meeting of the Estates General, to support four missionaries.

Even so, neither missionary work nor colonization flourished in the next few years. The Recollets circulated a memorial in France declaring that to convert the Indians it was necessary to increase the colony, "the greatest obstacle to which was on the part of the gentlemen of the Company, who, to monopolize trade, did not wish the country to be settled, and did not even wish us to make the Indians sedentary, without which nothing can be done for the salvation of these heathen."[14] The Recollet historian Leclercq also remarked of the Company that they were "very zealous for their trade," and that "they care little to deserve God's blessing by contributing to the interests of His glory."[15] Colonization and missionary activity were both expensive and incompatible with the trade, and the Company would do no more than provide free passage for two missionaries.

Moreover, as the Indians lost their fear of white men, Indian diplomacy took an increasing amount of Champlain's time. In 1622 the Iroquois sent ambassadors proposing a general peace. Champlain feared treachery and sent Montagnais ambassadors to get guarantees from the Iroquois. A peace treaty was satisfactorily negotiated, despite the opposition of some of the traders who felt that if peace were made the Iroquois would induce the Hurons to trade with the Dutch. In fact the Iroquois came with thirty-five canoes to trade at the Rapids in 1624. Champlain took good care of his commercial fences, sending Fathers Le Caron and Viel, Brother Sagard, and eleven other Frenchmen to winter with the Hurons in 1623, while Etienne Brûlé and two others wintered with the Algonquins.

Some Montagnais visited the Dutch during the winter of 1626-27 and reported that they had been invited to join the Mohicans in war against the Iroquois. Champlain opposed this alliance since it would strengthen his Dutch rivals. He tried to convince the Indians that peace was better than war, but some young hotheads raided the Iroquois in June and brought back prisoners for torture. Champlain persuaded them to release the prisoners and to send a deputation to seek pardon from the Iroquois for breaking the peace. But the ambassadors, who included a Frenchman, were promptly tortured and put to death by the Iroquois; thus the ancient war was resumed. While the Indians became more unruly, murdering two cowherds at Cap Tourmente near Quebec, Father Lalemant was forced to send most of his company back to France in the fall of 1627 when Jesuit recruits and supplies failed to arrive. This left only two priests in Quebec and Father Brébeuf with the Hurons. The blockade of the St. Lawrence by the English cut off supplies from France in 1628 and 1629, and finding no trade goods at Quebec, the Indians took their furs back home or to Fort Orange. The Dutch fur trade nearly doubled between 1626 and 1628, and quadrupled before the French came back to Quebec in 1632,[16] although the English are reported to have taken £300,000 worth of furs from Quebec in 1630. After twenty-one years of effort the French were left with nothing except their expertise in Indian relations.

However, when the French returned to Quebec, after the Treaty of St.-Germain-en-Laye, they had stronger backing in France than they had had before. Cardinal Richelieu had given the Jesuits the exclusive right to the mission of New France, since they were financially better able to undertake it than the Recollets. The sons of St. Ignatius Loyola now launched a vigorous missionary effort that continued to expand until 1690—unlike their earlier efforts in Acadia and at Quebec which had come to grief because of rivalry among Huguenot and Catholic traders and because they had duplicated the Recollets' efforts. Until 1663 the Jesuits dominated the life of New France, secular as well as religious, as Champlain had dominated it in the earlier period. Thanks to their connections in high places at court, they received the support in manpower and funds which the early trading companies and the Recollets had lacked. They came close to their goal of founding a Christian theocracy, where European and savage would live together in peace. They sought to convert the Indians for both God and king, so that "mingled with French traders and French settlers, softened by French manners, guided by French priests, ruled by French officers, their now divided bands would become the constituents of a vast wilderness empire, which in time might span the continent."[17]

As for intermarriage, Champlain had welcomed it. When he was visited by Indians at the site of Quebec he told them that after the proposed new settlement was established at the Lachine Rapids, "then our young men will marry your daughters, and we shall be one people."[18] Intermarriage had in fact already begun; of four recorded marriages at Quebec between 1604 and 1627, two were those of Frenchmen who espoused "squaws who were educated in our language and manners, and who have since persevered in great understanding, peace, and union with their husbands."[19] In Acadia young Latour had a daughter by a Micmac in 1626, and other illicit unions must have been numerous because of the acute scarcity of Frenchwomen. The Jesuits did their best to maintain strict morality in the settlements, but the *coureurs de bois* clearly followed the free sexual ways of their Indian hosts. Lescarbot is the only French writer of the period to censure such unions on racist grounds, remarking that "one ought not to mix Christian blood with infidel. . . ."[20]

French expansionism was marked from the early days of this second beginning of New France. In 1634 Champlain sent the interpreter Jean Nicolet, who had lived among the Algonquins, Nipissings, and Hurons, to visit the Puants (Onipigons) who were reputed to live by a western sea. Nicolet took with him a richly embroidered Chinese robe, in case he should reach the Orient by way of that sea, but the sea turned out to be Lake Michigan. Nicolet got no farther than Green Bay, which was to become an important French fur-trading center. There Nicolet concluded a treaty with the Indians and went on to discover the Fox River, which he explored as far as the village of the Mascoutins before returning to Quebec.

The work of the missions prospered; the twenty-two baptisms of 1635 were eclipsed by more than a hundred the following year. The numbers went on increasing each year, both along the St. Lawrence and in Huronia, where, by 1640, more than a thousand baptisms had taken place. At first the sacrament was administered chiefly to infants and the dying, but gradually healthy adult Indians demanded it too, though perhaps more as a matter of magical health insurance than of faith. In 1635 the Jesuits started teaching both French and Montagnais children at Quebec; two years later they were teaching Hurons and Algonquins as well. Now that the missionaries were favored rather than frowned upon by the civil authorities and had made some progress in the Indian languages, they found that the harvest of souls went much faster. "In contemplating the progress of the affairs of New France," LeJeune noted in 1636, "I seem to see dawn rising from the profound shadows of the night."[21]

Funds were made available in France for establishing a hospital, a school for Indian girls, and a seminary for Montagnais, Algonquins, and Hurons (for the missionaries now desired native helpers) at Quebec. The religious orders in France burned with zeal for the mission of New France. When the Hospital Nuns of Dieppe were asked for volunteers, all wanted to come, and prayers for the success of the mission were said night and day by other religious orders. In 1637, the Huron seminary was launched with six pupils.

By 1638 LeJeune could report that superstition, error, barbarism, and sin were being attacked by four means: war was made upon the enemy on his own ground with his own weapons, the Montagnais, Algonquin, and Huron tongues; a hospital was being built at Quebec to care for sick Indians, thanks to the Duchesse d'Aiguillon; the Huron, Algonquin, and Montagnais seminaries at Quebec were launched; and the effort to make the Indians sedentary was begun with the establishment of two Indian families on land near Quebec, thanks to the generosity of the Chevalier de Sillery. Thus the Jesuits of New France adopted the expedient, which later served them so well in Paraguay, of gathering their converts into villages where they could be instructed in agriculture and various trades, as well as in religion. The "reductions" of Paraguay were theocracies, governed by priests, and the Jesuits of New France did their best to achieve the same status for their establishments at Sillery, Trois-Riviéres, and, later, at Lorette and Caughnawaga. Here their flock could be guarded against corruption by the lawless *coureurs de bois* (who had adopted Indian ways instead of becoming intermediaries between cultures as Champlain had hoped) or unruly French soldiers. In 1639 Madame de la Peltrie brought three Ursuline nuns to establish a girls' school at Quebec, and three Hospital Nuns arrived to run the hospital. The Jesuit newcomers were so numerous that LeJeune referred to them as a "College of Jesuits." To top all, the Company helped his plan of settling the Indians by giving converts the same rights at its stores as Frenchmen and by providing cleared lands as dowries for young Indian girls.

The project of founding a colony at Montreal arose from the popularity of Champlain's *Voyages* and the *Jesuit Relations* in pious circles in France. The *Jesuit Relations* were annual reports of the mission of New France, written by the superior and incorporating the observations of all the missionaries. They were published each year from 1632 to 1674 and were intended for public consumption and designed to obtain support for the missions. They were truthful propaganda, feeding French curiosity about the Indians and the New World, and spurring pious zeal for the conversion of the savages. As early as 1640 it was observed that "a great part of France awaits [them] with some interest."[22] Increasingly they became appeals for special needs as well as reports of the work of the missions. They constitute a uniquely valuable source for Indian and French colonial

life in the seventeenth century. Even the anti-Jesuit Parkman regarded them as "authentic and trustworthy documents."[23] He used
them extensively in his great history, and much of the eloquence and
color of his narrative derives from these notably readable sources,
which helped to establish the later European concept of the "noble
savage."

About 1630 Jérôme Le Royer de La Dauversière, the Jesuit-
educated son of a tax collector, formed the notion of founding a
community of nuns to conduct a hospital for the Indians on the Island of Montreal, which nominally belonged to Jean de Lauzon,
head of the Company of New France. About the same time the Abbé
Jean-Jacques Olier, pastor of St. Sulpice in Paris, decided to work for
the conversion of the Indians of New France. The two men met by
chance and agreed to combine their efforts. Olier formed the Society
of Notre-Dame-de-Montréal, an association of pious laymen, to
which de Lauzon granted the Island of Montreal. The society was
not concerned with commerce, but existed only to "serve God and
the savages." It proposed to establish both a hospital and a seminary
at Montreal, but realized that the colony would have to fight for its
life against "the enemies of God and the State." Father Charles
Lalemant, who had returned to France to become the superior of the
Jesuits at Paris, chose the military leader for the new colony, Paul de
Chomedey, Sieur de Maisonneuve, a pious veteran of the Flemish
wars who burned with the desire to go to Canada "to serve God and
the king." Meanwhile Jeanne Mance, a young girl who had been
filled with missionary zeal by reading the *Relations*, persuaded the
Marquise de Bullion to provide the necessary funds for establishing
the new settlement. In 1640 twenty tons of provisions and materials
were sent out, and the next year Maisonneuve followed with forty
men and three ships. Governor Montmagny and the Jesuits finally
persuaded him to content himself with a preliminary reconnaissance
of Montreal that fall, though he was resolved to settle there "were
every tree on the island changed into an Iroquois."[24] As soon as the
ice was out of the St. Lawrence, Maisonneuve and his party set out
from Quebec for Montreal. On May 17, 1642, he received formal
possession of the island from Montmagny, and Father Vimont, the

Jesuit superior, said Mass. In his sermon Vimont observed: "What you see here is but a grain of mustard seed but . . . I have no doubt that this seed will produce a great tree; that it will one day work wonders, multiply itself, and spread out in all directions."[25] The Jesuit proved a good prophet.

The Iroquois grew ever more aggressive, and Montmagny set about building a fort at the mouth of the Richelieu to block their invasion path. The workers were attacked, but the Iroquois were driven off. In 1644 the Iroquois again terrorized New France. For a third year the Jesuits were unable to get their supplies through to Huronia. In May 1645 the governor sent a message to the Iroquois that the French would free their prisoners if the Iroquois were disposed to make a universal peace. Two chiefs appeared and offered wampum to settle their differences with the French. A truce was concluded on the condition that the Iroquois would take no hostile measures against the Hurons or other French allies until the chiefs of those nations had negotiated with them. Such meetings took place in the fall and again in the spring of 1646. Under the prodding of Montmagny, a general peace was concluded.

Almost immediately it was broken. Fort Richelieu, left unguarded, was destroyed in the fall of the same year. The Algonquins at Trois-Riviéres were attacked the next spring, and Montreal was subject to raiding parties. However, in 1648-49 the Iroquois directed most of their war parties against the Hurons. They burned the Huron towns and tortured the Jesuit missionaries to death. Thousands of Hurons were killed, and even more died of hunger after the devastation of their country. A few survivors reached Quebec in 1650, and the French established a village for them on the Ile d'Orléans. Other fugitive Hurons joined the colony until it numbered about six hundred souls. Another five hundred fugitives settled near Lake Superior. These were all that remained of the nation which once had numbered thirty thousand.

In the fall of 1651 Maisonneuve went to France to seek reinforcements for beleaguered Montreal. The tiny settlement was attacked in his absence but survived, thanks to the bravery of Lambert Closse. The return in September 1653 of Maisonneuve with 115 young and robust recruits—chosen for their skill in useful trades as well as in arms—restored the courage of the whole colony. The arrival of these newcomers marked the solid establishment of Montreal. Lands were cleared and new houses built, and the defenses of the town were greatly strengthened.

Undaunted, the Mohawks continued to make raids on both Montreal and Quebec. One of their demands was for the Hurons to join them and be absorbed into one nation. Some of the Hurons accepted this fate, and the French felt unable to prevent them from doing so. Finally, in 1657, Maisonneuve acted by confining all the Iroquois at Montreal. His action was also followed at Quebec, and the safe return of all the French missionaries then among the Iroquois was demanded. The Iroquois did not intend to comply, but the next spring the French at Onondaga managed to escape. The new governor, D'Argenson, wanted to lead a military force against the Iroquois, but could not muster sufficient numbers. He had to resort to diplomacy, but this too failed.

The French were now convinced that they must "either exterminate the Iroquois or see the colony fall." In 1659 they had begun to let their Algonquin allies burn captive Iroquois at the stake at Trois-Riviéres and Quebec. D'Argenson sent a dispatch to the king urging that troops be sent to protect the colony. He favored an initial attack on the Mohawks, who had received firearms from the Dutch and were the promoters of the war against the French. Declaring that the colony could only put into the field a hundred men, he urged that troops, provisions, and munitions be sent out from France. The Jesuits joined their pleas for troops with those of the governor so that France might "open Heaven to an infinity of savages; give life to this colony; conserve her New France, and acquire glory worthy of a very Christian kingdom."[26] Father Le Jeune was sent to France to support the cause at court. Meanwhile the colonists built small boats suitable for an expedition against the Iroquois, which they hoped might be launched the following year since France was now at peace in Europe. The much-desired troops did not arrive in New France until 1665, however, and the colonists had to suffer the usual cycle of Iroquois ambushes and Iroquois ambassadors seeking a peace which was no sooner made than broken.

Finally, Louis XIV, at the outset of his personal reign, under-

77

took the reorganization of the colony, which had so long struggled along as best it could under the administration of viceroys and merchants more concerned with the fur trade than with colonization and more eager for personal profit than for the welfare of the colony. Reiterated pleas for aid from France had been ignored by a government preoccupied with internal politics and European wars. But now the golden age of the colony dawned. With the institution of royal government, the mission of New France was launched and the Iroquois threat averted.

Thus in the early days of New France, before the institution of royal government in 1663, the pattern of French relations with the Indians was set. For the rest of the French régime in Canada French missionaries sought to civilize the Indians and to Frenchify them in peacetime; thanks to their efforts, in time of war the French found vitally needed allies in their underdog struggle with the English for domination in North America. Only the Iroquois were dependable allies of the English, and from time to time even they showed a remarkable ability to play off the English against the French in their own interest. Cadwallader Colden's *History of the Five Indian Nations Depending on the Province of New-York in America* is the only classic English work on the Indians to be written in the colonial period, and it lacks both the penetration and the sympathy which are to be found in the great mass of French material from Jacques Cartier to Contrecoeur. Even in the midst of the final disaster of New France, the last French governor took pains to provide for the Indians both politically and spiritually. Article 40 of the Capitulation of Montreal in September 1760 reads:

> The savages or Indian allies of his most Christian Majesty shall be maintained in the lands they inhabit, if they chuse to remain there; they shall not be molested on any pretense whatsoever, for having carried arms, and served his most Christian Majesty; they shall have, as well as the French, liberty of religion, and shall keep their missionaries. The actual Vicars General, and the Bishop, when the Episcopal See shall be filled, shall have leave to send to them new missionaries when they shall judge it necessary.

Jeffrey Amherst's gloss on these stipulations of Vaudreuil was:

"Granted, except the last article, which has been already refused."
He had already declined to leave the nomination of a bishop in the
power of the French king and to continue the bishop's existing
powers, which were forbidden under the English law of the time. But
the British honored this agreement to protect the Indians and attempted to create a vast reserve for them between the Ohio and the
Mississippi under the Proclamation of 1763. Though British and
American merchants took over the Montreal fur trade, it continued
to be carried on in the *pays-d'en-haut* largely by French Canadian
and *Métis* traders and voyageurs. Their working language was French
and they enjoyed far greater esteem among the Indians than did the
Scots of the Hudson's Bay Company. They demanded and received
French-speaking missionaries from Quebec and France. The French
fur trade created the "New Nation" in the West, the *Métis*, who
twice struck back in the latter part of the nineteenth century against
the westward moving tide of English-Protestant agricultural settlement which threatened their semi-nomadic way of life with its
French and Catholic traditions. Their leader in 1869-70 and 1885,
the tragic half-mad Louis Riel, justifiably called himself the "foun-
der of Manitoba" at his trial for treason. Riel is now generally recognized by English and French Canadians alike as a national hero, the
champion of a dying primitive way of life who fought valiantly
against the inevitable triumph of a more utilitarian form of civilization, which had little use for French, Catholic, or Indian values.

On balance, it is hard to quarrel with Parkman's verdict that
"French civilization embraced and cherished" the Indian. If it did so
in its own interest, which is clearly true, it is equally true that the
French also were moved by higher concerns which transcended—
uniquely among the European colonizing powers in North America—the national interest. Or perhaps in the last analysis they did
not, for there is a persistent French conviction, exemplified by General de Gaulle today, that "*Gesta Dei per Francos*,"—God's work is
done by the French.

NOTES

1– Francis Parkman, *The Jesuits in North America* (Boston, 1867), 1:131.

2– H. P. Biggar, *The Voyages of Jacques Cartier* (Ottawa, 1924), pp. 64-65.

3– *Brief Récit et succincte narration de la navigation faite en MDXXXV et MDXXXVI . . .* (Paris, 1863),pp. 5-6, 25-27, 31a.

4– *Edits, Ordonnances royaux, déclarations et arrêts du conseil d'état du roi concernant le Canada,* 3 vols. (Quebec, 1854-56), 1:3, 5-6.

5– H. P. Biggar, ed., *A Collection of Documents Relating to Jacques Cartier* (Ottawa, 1930), p. 77.

6– Ibid., pp. 70-72.

7– Biggar, *The Voyages of Jacques Cartier*, p. 256.

8– R. G. Thwaites, ed., *The Jesuit Relations and Allied Documents* (Cleveland, 1896-1901), 5:63, 195.

9– "Cadillac Papers," *Michigan Pioneer & Historical Collections* (1904), 30:99, 166-67.

10– H. P. Biggar, ed., *The Works of Samuel de Champlain* (Toronto, 1922), 1:152.

11– Thwaites, *Jesuit Relations*, 3:105.

12– Biggar, *Works of Champlain*, 1:231.

13– Ibid., 3:16.

14– Leclerq, quoted by Morris Bishop, *Champlain: The Life of Fortitude* (New York, 1948), p. 264.

15– Ibid., quoting Leclerq, p. 264.

16– G. T. Hunt, *The Wars of the Iroquois* (Madison, Wis., 1960), p. 33.

17– Parkman, *Jesuits*, 1:131.

18– Thwaites, *Jesuit Relations*, 5:211.

19– Leclerq, *Premier Etablissement de la foy dans la Nouvelle France* (Paris, 1691), 1:223.

20– Marc Lescarbot, *History of New France* (Toronto, 1914), 3:167.

21– Thwaites, *Jesuit Relations*, 9:133.

22– Ibid., 18:60.

23– Parkman, *Jesuits*, 1:vi.

24– R. Flenley, ed., Dollier de Casson, *A History of Montreal, 1640-1672* (New York, 1928), p. 91.

25– Ibid., p. 99.

26– Thwaites, *Jesuit Relations*, 45:201.

British-Colonial Attitudes and Policies Toward the Indian in the American Colonies

Wilbur R. Jacobs

A participant at a recent conference on American Indian history, held at the University of California, Los Angeles, urged that Indian history be written from the Indian point of view. Interviewers equipped with tape recorders should record contemporary Indian viewpoints—such tape recordings would disclose how the Indians themselves regard their past. "This," urged the U.C.L.A. speaker, "is the most sorely neglected area of Indian history."[1] A number of scholars participating in the conference expressed a similar point of view. Obviously students acquainted with the field are not altogether satisfied that an accurate account of Indian history emerges from the literature presently available. "What is the truth in the history of the Indian and the white people?" asked a leading scholar from the Smithsonian Institution.[2]

Certainly this truth is not easy to uncover, as a glance at the wide range of opinion and interpretation in this field of early American history makes clear. The article on Indians in the *Large Soviet Encyclopedia*, for instance, paints a particularly black picture of this segment of our history, emphasizing the brutality of the English settlers in Indian-white affairs. The first colonists are portrayed as rapacious invaders: "The original development of America's native population was disrupted by the intrusion of European colonizers. The entire history of embattled America is one of unheard-of violence and treachery, of mass destruction of native peoples and their enslavement. The Indians resisted in despair but were defeated."[3]

The theme of Anglo-American maltreatment of the Indians permeates almost all Soviet accounts of United States history and is the dominant theme in Soviet histories dealing with the early American frontier. My initial reaction to this point of view, which I first encountered some years ago while writing an article on the Soviet image of American history,[4] was one of rejection. I resented what I regarded as an inaccurate and unfair account of early American history in which the colonists were depicted as greedy, selfish invaders who exterminated Indians in order to take possession of the land. Yet further study of Indian history (and of the writings of others who have studied the subject) has convinced me that there is, unfortunately, much truth in the Soviet encyclopedia account. It is only too easy to brand as propaganda writings which reject our own fond myths about our attitudes and policies. But the history which caters to our self-love is no history at all. It is time that we resisted the urge to blot out our uncomfortable pages of colonial Indian history so that the full story may be told.

If the history of Indian-white relations in colonial America is not one we can be proud of, we must also recognize that this is not a simple story to tell. This is a subject of considerable complexity, for the various colonies differed widely in the policies they adopted toward the Indians. The friendliness of the Pilgrims toward the Wampanoag and Massachusetts tribes, which had suffered population losses in an epidemic of 1616-19, was different from the attitudes of John Smith and his fellow Virginians toward Powhatan, leader of a confederacy of some thirty tribes.[5] Nor is there a clear-cut pattern of Indian relationships in the proprietary colonies. Quaker-Indian relationships, for example, are unique in terms of the orderly manner in which land was occupied and the care which was taken to maintain friendly relations with adjacent tribes.[6] The Carolinians, by contrast, ruthlessly enslaved many Indian captives who fell into their hands.[7]

The Indian superintendency system, set up in 1755, represented a high point in British efforts to exercise more effective control over all relations with the Indians. In a number of the colonies, however, headstrong governors and powerful legislative committees quarreled with each other in an effort to maintain control of Indian policy, especially in matters pertaining to the fur and skin trade or defense. The new imperial system sought to create a greater centralization of authority with two superintendents, one in the north and one in the south, each extending his authority over an extensive area.[8] The effectiveness of these imperial officers, however, was much reduced by the interference of colonial governors and by the refusal of provincial assemblies to subsidize expensive gifts for the Indians. Eventually, the mother country took the initiative in furnishing money to be used for presents in an effort to win Indian allegiance in the final stages of the French and Indian War.

The postwar decision of Sir Jeffrey Amherst, commander in chief of the British forces in America, to discontinue such subsidies to the natives was partly responsible for the Indian uprising of 1763 under Pontiac.[9] Amherst's suggestions, that the Indians be hunted down with large dogs and that blankets used by smallpox victims be presented to Indian warriors, illustrate the hostility of some of the men who were responsible for carrying out British Indian policy.[10] Indeed, much of our colonial Indian history twitches and throbs with incidents of inhumanity. Fortunately not all British policy makers were as vicious and as short-sighted as Amherst, and British policy did, on occasion, attempt to protect the Indians. At the end of the French and Indian War Britain attempted to halt western expansion by issuing the Proclamation of 1763, and, in a series of treaties concluded with western tribes (in 1764, 1768, and 1775), attempted to set boundary lines that would satisfy land speculators and bring about an orderly occupation of the frontier.[11] Regulations concerning land purchases and trade with the Indians also showed Britain's increasing concern for the Indian. These measures, however, proved ineffectual. The frontiersmen and the land speculators had, in the years from 1763 to 1775, become far more independent. Eager for frontier lands, they were not at all ready to accept regulations imposed by the British. Not unexpectedly they joined the Revolutionaries in the War of Independence.[12]

Throughout the colonial period the mother country had had no real choice but to permit a large degree of colonial control over Indian affairs. Confronted with the increasing demands of semi-independent commonwealths in North America, the British frequently did not possess the power to enforce their authority over far-reaching wilderness frontiers. Nor is there much evidence to show that the English, before the 1750s, were particularly interested in Indians other than as providers of lands and furs or as auxiliaries in fighting the French and Spaniards.

A wide assortment of contemporary records reveals that the seventeenth-century colonials, who helped mold early Indian policy, generally considered themselves superior to the aborigines. The first settlers' writings often record that they were repelled by Indian religion, Indian sexual mores, Indian illiteracy, and Indian ideas of dress, personal modesty, and adornment.[13] There are frequent portrayals of Indians as depraved, savage brutes, as impious rascals who lived in filth and ate nasty food.[14] Even Francis Parkman, one of the first serious students of the Indian, portrayed him in colonial history as a savage of the Stone Age whose homicidal fury in war gave him a demoniac character.[15]

There is evidence that seventeenth- and eighteenth-century colonials tended not only to despise the Indian but also to hate and distrust him. By tradition, Europeans associated the "heathen" or "infidel" with warfare and conflict, and the primitive Indian was expected to be hostile. Sometimes Indian friendliness was actually viewed with suspicion; such friendliness might well mask deceit and treachery. As Wilcomb Washburn points out, the almost atavist fear of Indian treachery can be traced back to Jamestown in 1607, when Christopher Newport recognized the friendliness of the natives, but commented that they were "naturally given to treachery."[16] This point of view later became a basic ingredient in the histories of Virginia. In 1898, for example, the historian Alexander Brown wrote that friendly Indians "probably boded the little colony a future harm."[17] There was in fact a widespread belief that Indians were enemies of the commonwealth. The saying, "The only good Indian is a dead Indian," owes its existence to this shrunken, distorted view of the natives.

The Puritan settlers were equally suspicious of the Indian. According to contemporary accounts, they seem often to have regarded acts of hospitality on his part as acts of God. Their prejudice was rooted in the morality of the Old Testament, which was refined and strengthened by historical phenomena such as the Pequot War. The assumption that the Indian was an obstacle to the progress of civilization made it difficult for the Puritans to recognize Indian virtue. Indian generosity was explained by God's intervention, for He had caused the Indians to behave temporarily in a benevolent fashion. In Puritan annals we therefore find such statements as, "God caused the Indians to help us with fish at very cheap rates. . . ."[18] Such bias toward the Indians was of course partly due to the fact that early Puritan fathers saw their life in the New World as a portion of a preordained plan, the unfolding of God's will. The natives were merely God's agents on earth. Thus the religious beliefs of the Puritans and many other colonials encouraged them to look on the tribesmen as part of the hostile environment of the New World. The Bible (particularly the Old Testament) continued to be used as a guide in Indian affairs. In the late eighteenth century, for instance, James Adair, a South Carolina Indian trader, concluded that the culture of the Southern Indians was a survival of customs from the ten lost tribes of Israel.[19]

The erroneous belief that the Indians were treacherous and unreliable persisted among British and provincials throughout the colonial period. English generals, such as Edward Braddock and Sir Jeffrey Amherst, exhibited this attitude, and, in 1763 under its influence, the Paxton Boys of the frontier hamlet of Pennsylvania butchered harmless Conestoga Indians. The fact that a number of the Christian "Moravian Indians" were housed in barracks in Philadelphia caused a spokesman for the Paxton rioters to write an angry "Remonstrance" to the governor of Pennsylvania and the Assembly: "The Indians now at Philadelphia are His Majesty's Perfidious Enemies, & therefore to protect and maintain them at Public Expense, while our suffering Brethren on the Frontiers are almost destitute of the necessaries of Life, and are neglected by the Public, is sufficient to make us mad with rage, and tempt us to do what nothing but the most violent necessity can vindicate."[20]

The colonials liked to regard the Indians as members of a nomadic hunting race with no fixed habitation, roaming over thousands of acres of virgin wilderness.[21] This wish-fulfilling dream of the nomadic Indian (which was later used as an excuse for taking Indian land—Presidents John Adams and Theodore Roosevelt, among others, made use of this argument) ignored the fact that many of the tribes of eastern North America lived in populous towns and villages (often called castles by the British). Such towns contained houses, streets, fortifications, centers for civic and religious events, as well as corn fields, orchards, and garden plots.[22] North American Indians were generally good fishermen, hunters, and farmers. Their society, with its complicated political and social customs, was not easily understood by the European; many Indian societies were in certain ways highly developed—in terms of occupational specialization, social controls, and class structure, for instance—but the colonials were generally content to remain ignorant of Indian society and had little reason to doubt their own superiority. The fact that the white man was better at making guns (blacksmiths had to be stationed in central Indian villages during the Seven Years' War) helped buttress their arrogant assumptions.[23]

Fortunately, some early explorers, as well as British officers and colonials, were free of the prejudice which tainted the judgment of the majority. We have available to us, therefore, a number of accounts of Indian generosity and benevolence. Among those who recognized Indian virtues were many of the Spanish explorers such as Christopher Columbus, Alvar Núñez Cabeza de Vaca, and Francisco de Coronado; such well-known figures as Jacques Cartier, John Smith, William Bradford, and Roger Williams also left favorable accounts of the Indians. The seventeenth-century Virginia Indians are described by contemporaries as "the most gentle loving faithful people . . . such as live after the manner of the golden age"; the Wampanoags, Bradford wrote, were "a speciall instrument of God."[24] Early missionaries praised the freedom-loving Indian who lived in a world untainted by the corruption of European society.

Robert Rogers, famed ranger, fighter, and Indian agent, and probably one of the best eighteenth-century judges of the Indian character, was full of praise for the Indians south of the Great Lakes: "These people of any upon earth seem blessed in this world; here is health and joy, peace and plenty; care and anxiety, ambition and the love of gold, and every uneasy passion, seem banished from this happy region."[25] Sir William Johnson, the Irish-born Northern Indian superintendent for the British who had married a Mohawk woman, Molly (Joseph Brant's sister), was no romantic idealist where Indians were concerned. His experience in frontier diplomacy, trade and land speculation exceeded that of any other British colonial official in the eighteenth century. Writing to a British scientist in 1771 about the Six Nations Iroquois, Johnson praised the sachems of the grand council at Onondaga for conducting their deliberations with "regularity and decorum." The speaker was never interrupted; harsh language was never used, no matter what the speaker may have been thinking at the time.[26] Moreover Johnson judged many Englishmen to be ignorant of the customs of the Indians which, if better known, would be admired and respected. In Johnson's words:

> On their haunts, as on all other occasions, they are strict observers of meum and tuum; and this from principle, holding theft in contempt; so that they are rarely guilty of it, though tempted by articles of much value. Neither do the strong attempt to seize the prey of the weak; and I must do them justice to say that, unless heated by liquor, or inflamed by revenge, their ideas of right and wrong and their practices in consequence of them, would if more known, do them much honour.[27]

Examples of colonial expressions of respect and admiration for the Indian can be multiplied. Various delegations of Indian chiefs who visited London in the eighteenth century were cordially received and much admired everywhere. Some of them were painted by Sir Joshua Reynolds. Copies of the paintings circulated throughout Britain, and a few of these survive as rare prints in Huntington Library vaults and in other libraries. British officers who had been among the Indians in America reinforced the favorable impression made by the chiefs. In June 1756, for example, a young British military officer, Charles Lee, recorded his impressions of the Indians for his sister in England. He had seen the Indians at their worst and had been with Braddock on the Monongahela, but he insisted that the sympathetic account of the Indians which Cadwallader Colden had given in his *History of the Five Nations* was "literally true." Of the Mohawks, the tribe of the Iroquois that he had come to know from personal experience, Lee wrote:

> I can assure you that they are a much better sort of people than commonly represented; they are hospitable, friendly and civil to an immense degree; in good breeding I think they infinitely surpass the French or any other people that I ever saw, if you will allow good breeding to consist in the constant desire to do ev'rything that will please you, and in strict carefulness not to do anything that may offend you. . . . [These warriors] acquire something of an ease and gracefulness in their walk and air which is not to be met with elsewhere, their Dress I like most wonderfully. . . . Their Complexion is deep olive, their eyes and teeth very fine, but their skins are most inexpressibly soft and silky. Their men are in general handsomer than their women, but I have seen some of them very pretty.[28]

Other comments on scalping and warfare may strike us as less flattering to the Indians, but it is clear that Lee is quite sincere in his praise of the Mohawks; indeed, he finally decided to marry a daughter of one of the Seneca chiefs, "a very great beauty." "You may think," he wrote his sister, "that I am endeavoring to make my letter Romantic but I give you my word and honour that it is every syllable facts."[29] Lee in later times turned against the Indians and, as a Revolutionary general, was accused of betraying the patriot cause. But for many years he kept in touch with his Indian wife who had borne him twins.

Edmond Atkin, Southern Indian superintendent, a man long experienced in the Indian trade before he took over the superintendency, gives us another favorable view of the Indians. In a long report addressed to the Board of Trade, Atkin had this to say about the Chickasaws:

The Chic[k]asaws are of all Indians the most Manly in their persons, Sentiments, and Actions; being of large graceful figure, open Countenance and Manners, and generous Principles; Vigorous, Active, Intrepid, and Sharp in appearance even to Fierceness; expert horsemen (having perhaps the finest breed of Horses in N. America); by much the best Hunters; and without Exception (by acknowledgement of all Europeans as well as Indians that know them, who respect them as such) the best Warriors. Even their Women handle Arms, and face the Enemy like Men.[30]

In this same report, Atkin made some general observations about the Indians along the British frontiers and their relations with the whites. "No people in the World," Atkin wrote,

understand and pursue their true National Interest, better than the Indians. How sanguinary soever they are towards their enemies, from a misguided Passion of Heroism, and love of their country; yet they are otherways truly humane, hospitable, and equitable. And how fraudulent soever they have been reputed, from the Appearance of their military Actions, in which according to their method of War, Glory cannot be acquired without Cunning and Stratagem; Yet in their publick Treaties no People on earth are more open, explicit, and Direct. Nor are they excelled by any in the observance of them.[31]

Thus the refutation of the various charges made against the Indians—that they were treacherous and barbaric, inferior to the white man—came from those who knew the Indian best: from the early explorers and missionaries, and later from soldiers and Indian agents. Moreover, a few colonials and British officers clearly recognized something akin to the noble savage in the Indian, though many years were to pass before the noble savage gained fame in French and American literature. The fictional Indians may in fact be less unrealistic, less romanticized, than we have assumed, their virtues based on those actually possessed by the native Americans. Modern scholars, however, seem to have rejected firsthand reports preferring to regard the nobility imputed to the Indian as a myth. This stubborn refusal to revise suspect opinions must make us fear that the old arrogance, the old need to blackwash the Indian, still exists among many scholars today.[32]

The favorable views of the Indians expressed during colonial times were unfortunately muted and finally all but smothered by the prevailing attitude of white superiority. Most colonials seem to have rejected the idea that the Indians could be absorbed into white society through intermarriage or assimilation.[33] Yet, at a later date, Thomas Jefferson thought that the Indians, after the passing of the frontier, might well become acculturated and adopt the white man's way of life, or at least his methods of agriculture.[34] In fact, however, tribes like the Conestoga in Pennsylvania—who survived in a sea of white settlements—were never assimilated into white society. There are scattered examples of Indians who attended the various colonial colleges, including Harvard and William and Mary (which set up a special program for the education of promising Indians), but not a single one seems to have made any mark on white society. Traders on the frontier occasionally had Indian wives. William Johnson is said to have had two after the death of his first wife. But there are surprisingly few known cases of mixed marriages between Indians and British colonials, although many Virginians have attempted to trace their ancestry back to John Rolfe and Pocahontas. Andrew Montour, the Indian interpreter of the middle colonies, is a rare example of a half-caste who attained some prominence. But his case is a special one, for his father was Iroquois, his mother Canadian (she too may have been the offspring of a mixed marriage). Although Montour seems to have been an illiterate, he was nevertheless a master of Indian dialects and was fluent in both English and French. The Moravian missionary, Count Zinzendorf, wrote the following description of Montour in 1742:

> Andrew's cast of countenance is decidedly European, and had not his face been encircled with a broad band of paint, applied with bear's fat, I would certainly have taken him for one. He wore a brown broadcloth coat, a scarlet damaskan lappel-waistcoat, breeches, over which his shirt hung, a black Cordovan neckerchief, decked with silver bubles, shoes stockings, and a hat. His ears were hung with pendants of brass and other wires plated together like the handle of a basket.[35]

Andrew owned property and demanded and received compensation for his services. One point seems to have distinguished him clearly from his Indian contemporaries: he wore European breeches. Though many items of clothing were given as presents to the Indians, breeches were never among them.

In the few recorded cases where children were born of unions between Indians and white settlers, the white mother was usually a prisoner who had been captured by the Indians in war. At the end of Pontiac's uprising, female captives were given the chance to return home to their families and white husbands, but many of the women preferred to remain with the Indians.[36] The rarity of such unions, then, was not the result of a natural antagonism between the two races, but rather of the barriers raised by the white man's belief in his own superiority.

William Christy Macleod in his perceptive volume, *American Indian Frontier*, gives us an insight into the practical obstacles to intermarriage:

> An Indian wife was an asset to the trader among the Indians. But the agricultural settlers, both French and British, did not want Indian women as wives. Farmers needed wives who knew the ways of European housekeeping and husbandry, who knew how to milk cows, fry eggs, and so on. The farmer, even in Virginia, so late as 1682, often preferred to pay the expense of importing women of questionable repute from European cities, at considerable cost, than to take Indian women who would be helpless on a farmer's homestead.[37]

The reluctance of the average British colonist to accept intermarriage with the Indians was, in the opinion of William Byrd of Westover, a basic cause for Indian-white conflict. Writing in his *History of the Dividing Line* in 1728, Byrd observed that the Indians "could, by no means, persuade themselves that the English were heartily their Friends, so long as they disdained to intermarry with them." If the colonists had been serious about converting and civilizing the Indians, Byrd said, "they would have ... brought their Stomachs to embrace this prudent alliance. ... For, after all that can be said, a sprightly Lover is the most prevailing Missionary that can be sent among these, or any other Infidels." Byrd suggested, with just a touch of irony, that the Indians might be prepared to give up their lands peacefully as a form of dowry if they were convinced that their daughters would be accepted as equals in white society.

Governor Alexander Spotswood, writing to the Lord Commissioners of Trade and Plantations in 1717, also commented on the absence of intermarriage:

> And as to beginning a nearer friendship by intermarriage (as the Custom of the French is), the inclinations of our people are not the same with those of that Nation, for not withstanding the long intercourse between ye inhabitants of this Country and ye Indians and their living amongst one another for so many Years, I cannot find one Englishman that has an Indian Wife, or an Indian marreyed to a white woman.[38]

The Board of Trade in England was displeased with this state of affairs and recommended to the king in 1721 that intermarriage be encouraged:

> It was for this reason, that, in the draught of Instructions for the Governor of Nova Scotia, we took the liberty of proposing to your majesty that proper encouragement should be given to such of your Majesty's subjects as should intermarry with the native Indians; and we conceive it might be for your majesty's service that the said instructions should be extended to all other British colonies.[39]

Even the Quakers and pacifist German sects in Pennsylvania seem to have rejected intermarriage, although they were interested in establishing friendly relations with the Indians. Penn's message to the Indians, sent before his arrival in Pennsylvania, was full of good will and friendship: "I have great Love and Regard toward you," he told the Indians, "and I desire to win and gain your Love and Friendship by a Kind, Just and Peaceful Life." The Indians seem to have accepted this message; they loved and respected Penn and trusted the Quakers, who were generous with gifts and treated them with fairness. It was not until the middle of the eighteenth century that Pennsylvania suffered the terror of Indian attack.[40] Penn's descendants had abandoned his faith and had adopted a far less humane policy toward the Indians than that of the first settlers; the Indians were cheated in land transactions and in trade, and exposed to the ravages of rum. In a complete reversal of the earlier policy, attempts were made to dominate the Indians by constructing forts rather than by giving presents. The original Quaker policy was defended by Superintendent Edmond Atkin who wrote that it was necessary "to begin building Forts in their hearts . . . after which we may build Forts wherever we please."[41]

Before extensive fortifications could be built along the wide Pennsylvania frontier, war broke out. In 1756, Lieutenant Governor Robert Hunter Morris and the Pennsylvania Council drew up a declaration of war providing for bounties for native scalps ($130 for a male over twelve years, $50 for a female). Although attempts were made to thwart this plan, it was, with the support of non-Quakers, pushed through the Council; the Assembly was consulted only after hostilities had commenced. Yet the Pennsylvania Assembly cannot be awarded a clean bill of health on the matter of scalp bounties. On July 4, 1764, following a proclamation of war against the Delaware and Shawnee Indians, the Assembly approved an elaborate scheme for scalp bounties for all "Enemy" Indians over the age of ten! This act marked the end of the era of friendly relations between Indians and whites in Pennsylvania.[42]

The imperial Indian superintendent, Edmond Atkin, spoke out forcibly against the barbaric practice of offering scalp bounties. He declared that the Earl of Loudoun, British commander in chief in the colonies in the late 1750s, "detests the practice." Such bounties, Atkin argued, encouraged what he called *"private scalping,* whereby the most innocent & helpless persons, even Women & Children, are properly murdered." Such a policy, Atkin asserted, was "only becoming the greatest Savages, & unworthy of any Christian people." Atkin also said that he had reason to believe that the royal governors had "been cautioned" to discourage the practice of giving "Rewards" for scalps. Atkin, who was, of course, interested in establishing the authority of the Indian superintendent, pointed out that Sir William Johnson never rewarded warriors specifically for bringing back scalps.[43]

Atkin's protests were futile, for, like a number of other imperial officers, he found himself at odds with colonial assemblies and colonial governors over the questions of policy and the implementing of policy. The authority which he claimed as an officer of the crown was frequently defied; like other imperial officers, and indeed the British Parliament, he found that the wishes of the crown oftentimes had little influence on the decisions of the colonials.

To make matters worse the imperial officers themselves often disagreed over Indian affairs. Governor William Shirley of Massachusetts had a long and bitter feud with William Johnson over questions of authority in dealing with the northern Indians, and Governor James Glen of South Carolina was responsible for calling a large conference of Cherokees at the very time when Governor Dinwiddie of Virginia had contracted with these same Indians (some five hundred warriors) to lead Braddock's army through the woods toward Fort Duquesne.[44] The course of colonial history might have been different if Glen had not insisted on having his way. Dinwiddie concluded that Governor Glen was "wrongheaded," but he, on his side, quarreled with Atkin about a "monsterous account" for Indian gifts, and he harassed his deputy, young George Washington, with detailed instructions for dealing with Indians. Washington found Atkin almost impossible to work with and finally decided to ignore the superintendent's instructions.[45] Muddle and strife were two of the main characteristics of British-Indian policy throughout most of the colonial period.

The lack of clarity in British policy may help to explain why the various colonies insisted on making their own decisions on questions related to their own Indians. Moreover, the authority of the British was challenged by the Indians as well as by the colonials. The Iroquois and other Indians declined to be referred to in treaties as "subjects" of the crown. They treated British officials and governors as equals and often gave them Indian names. Virginia's governor was called Brother Assaraquoa. Brother Onas was the name for the governor of Pennsylvania, and Maryland's governor had a special name, Brother Tocarry-Hogan, to denote his geographical position between the neighboring colonies. Significantly, the Indians did not use the term "Father" in addressing the English as they sometimes did in treaty talks with Count Frontenac, who insisted on this title (although the Iroquois perhaps humored him by using it).

To understand exactly what the colonists and the British government wanted from the Indians, we cannot do better than take a careful look at the terms of one or two fairly representative British-Indian treaties. The Pettaquamscut Treaty of July 15, 1675, was concluded between Major Thomas Savage (not an inappropriate name) and his fellow officers, representing Massachusetts and Connecticut, and the various sachems of the friendly Narragansett Indians. The main terms were as follows: (1) The sachems were to deliver King Philip's subjects "dead or alive." (2) All "stolen property" was to be returned to the whites. (3) Disputes over property where the case was not clear were to be judged by "impartial men." (4) Pilfering and "acts of hostility" toward the English "shall for the future forever cease." (5) Certain chiefs were to be held as hostages to insure peace. (6) The award for the capture of Philip alive was two coats; for his head, one coat. (7) All land grants, sales, bargains, conveyances of lands, meadow, timber, grass, stones "bought or quietly possessed" by the English were renewed, confirmed "forever." (8) "God" was called "to witness that they [the Indians] were and would in the future remain true friends of the English."[46]

The hard terms of this treaty would scarcely lead one to suspect what was actually the case—that the Indian partners to the treaty were friendly towards the whites. What the Puritan fathers wanted was the death or capture of their enemy; the protection and restoration of the Puritan settlers' property; and finally, approval for their occupation and possession of land—to all of which God was to act as witness. When the Narragansett tribesmen did not live up to the letter of this demanding treaty, the Puritans (aware of the value of the Narragansett land) launched a vicious attack against them.[47]

Another representative Indian treaty which tells us much about the development of Indian policy took place almost a century later. The Treaty of Logstown of 1752 was agreed to by the British government, the Ohio Company of Virginia, and several individual colonies on the one hand, and by the Ohio Iroquois and other tribes on the other hand. The demands made were somewhat similar to those of the Pettaquamscut Treaty, but this agreement covered a far greater territory; the British laid claim to almost the whole Ohio Valley. After elaborate preparations, including the transportation of what was said to be the largest gift of goods ever presented to the Indians, the sachems were persuaded to ratify older treaties giving the British ownership of a large part of the upper Middle West. The whites piously defended the "pen and ink work" of the almost certainly fraudulent treaties, but Half King, an Iroquois sachem, protested: "We never understood, until you told us Yesterday, that the Lands then sold were to extend further to the sun setting, than the Hill on the other side of the Alleghany Hill."[48] The conference was a friendly one with the whites listening to Indian complaints, yet on questions of land ownership the whites won on every point.

Land was not the only concern at this meeting. The commissioners tried to calm Indian anger over fur trade abuses, to warn the Indians about French duplicity, and to cultivate Iroquois friendship with presents and fine speeches. Inquiries about an Indian murderer were made, and the question of religious instruction for the Indians was raised. The conference was, from the white point of view, successful, for within a few years the Iroquois tribesmen were allying themselves with the British against the French.

At a great Indian conference held at the headquarters of William Johnson in June 1755, Iroquois warriors were recruited for a campaign against the French at Lake George. The Logstown Treaty had helped to smooth the way for this later conclave. Extant minutes of the conference detail the arrival of group after group of warriors until finally the Mohawks and their missionary came on the evening of June 21, 1755. "At Dinner time," according to the minutes, "the Sachems & warriors of the hither Mohawk Castle March'd to Col. Johnson's with the Revd. Mr. [John] Ogilvie their Missionary & their chief Sachem at their Head & made a fine appearance."[49]

These three conferences cover a time span of a hundred years.[50] They document an overwhelming greed for land; both colonists and crown officials were prepared to fight for it, pay something for it, or cheat for it. Next the whites wanted the Indians' services. If they could not win them as allies, they wanted them as mercenary soldiers, and in the later colonial period they paid certain tribesmen in money to fight for them. The colonials were also prepared to make use of forced labor. King Philip's wife and child, for instance, were sold into slavery, and Verner Crane in *The Southern Frontier* reports on the hundreds of Indian women and children sold into slavery in South Carolina.[51] A doctoral dissertation on the law and the Indian in the colony of Massachusetts Bay reveals that Indian slaves were used by the Puritans as well.[52] Boston newspapers carried advertisements for the capture of runaway Carolina Indian slaves. Local New England Indians were also enslaved or hired from jails to act as servants. Sometimes they were assigned to reservations called "villages" where, if they did not revolt, they were forced to live under a stern code of law that discriminated against minorities—Negro, mulatto, and Indian. "Free Indians" were sometimes settled on the frontier, where they acted as a buffer between the inhabitants of the state and external enemies. The "wild" Indians of the frontier were left to their own devices until disease, war, or other factors left them weak enough to be brought under the legal jurisdiction of the whites.[53] In South Carolina, soldiers and allied Indians on slave-catching raids plundered the Spanish mission towns of Appalache tribesmen who were unarmed and easy victims for the Carolina slavers.[54] A census of 1708 recorded 1,400 Indian slaves in South Carolina, about half the number of Negro slaves.[55]

Thus the Indian served the colonial whites as warrior, servant or slave. But this was not all; he also served them as a hunter, as a procurer of furs. At Logstown and other treaty conclaves there were attempts to rectify the worst abuses of the fur traders (called by Governor Dinwiddie the "abandoned wretches" of the frontier), but there was no attempt to discontinue the trade because it was considered vital to imperial economic life. A play written by Robert Rogers, *Ponteach: or the Savages of America, A Tragedy* (published in London in 1766), depicts the unsavory side of the trade, showing how the trading fraternity justified its outrageous conduct. In the first act, McDole, an old hand at the trade, instructs Murphey, a beginner:

> McDole: So, Murphey, you are come to try your Fortune Among the
> Savages in this wild Desart?
> Murphey: Ay any thing to get an honest living. . . . I've Rum and Blan-
> kets, Wampum, Powder, Bells, And such Trifles they're want to prize.

McDole: 'Tis very well: your Articles are good: But now the Thing's to
make a profit from them, Worth all your Toil and Pains of coming
hither. Our fundamental Maxim then is this,
That it's no Crime to cheat and gull an Indian.
Murphey: How! Not a Sin to cheat an Indian, say you? Are they not
Men? hav'nt they a Right to Justice As well as we, though savage in
their manners?
McDole: Ah! If you boggle here, I say no more;
This is the very Quintessence of the trade. . . .[56]

Rogers' play mirrors the arrogant spirit of the fur trade and
the open manner in which the Indians were cheated. Sir William
Johnson's long catalogue of traders' sins shows that McDole's statement in the play, "it's no Crime to cheat and gull an Indian," is no
exaggeration of the attitude prevalent among the traders. The few
missionaries who ventured among the Indians did not share this
view, but even a man like the Reverend John Ogilvie (an Anglican
missionary among the Mohawks and a member of the Society for the
Propagation of the Gospel in Foreign Parts) tried to persuade the
Indians to fight against the French. Ogilvie, who wanted to win the
Mohawks to the British cause, resembled those Canadian priests in
the eighteenth century who helped to lead "praying Indians" against
the New England towns.[57]

British officials and colonists demanded a great deal from the
Indian—his land, his services as warrior, servant, slave, or procurer of
furs, and, sometimes, his soul. In return the Indians were given various types of goods, including arms, utensils, clothing, blankets, and
food—and rum and disease. If the Indian did not cooperate, he was
pushed out of the way. The proclamation line of 1763 was, as
George Washington pointed out, a temporary expedient "to quiet
the minds of the Indians." Most colonials were simply not interested
in justice for the Indians. It was enough that they be kept quiet.

Official British policy was unsuccessful, but it was, at least in
its intentions, oftentimes humane in outlook. The extreme unsuit-
ability of many of those appointed to implement British policy may
lead us to assume that the policy itself was more vicious than was
actually the case. Late in the eighteenth century, however, the British were able to bring about a whole series of reforms in Canada de-

signed to protect the Indian and give him some sanctuary. The success of that policy led to the relatively peaceful occupation of the Canadian west.

It is difficult to know who or what was responsible for the disastrous treatment accorded the Indians during the American colonial period. Certainly the ignorance of the colonists concerning the culture of the native tribes made it possible for them to regard the Indians as inferior to themselves. And their prejudice, in turn, made it easier for them to acquiesce to, or actually take part in, the maltreatment of the Indians. The situation is not without modern parallels to other cases of widespread racial or religious prejudice—in Nazi Germany, in South Africa, or even in America today.

But the whole weight of blame cannot be placed on the settlers. If British policy makers had been firm in their resolve to protect the Indian, the situation might have been different. In fact, however, British policy was frequently weak and ineffectual. Corrupt governors like Lord Cornbury gave away whole sections of western New York in order to pocket patent fees, and were rarely disciplined or removed from office.[58] In short, there was no important body of imperial law for the protection of the Indians and their lands.

The immediate causes of violence, however, lay not so much in the underlying societal factors already discussed—an ignorant and prejudiced white population, a negligent and ineffectual imperial authority—but in the tinderbox atmosphere at the points of contact: in the wilderness and, especially, at the cutting edge of the provincial agricultural frontier. The whites were greedy for furs and land, and, far from established authority, they were not frequently inhibited by a fear of the law. The Indians, cheated by the whites in trade and treaties, saw their hunting grounds encroached upon and their very lives endangered. Indians and whites alike were inflamed and one atrocity provoked another. Liquor, disease, and firearms helped to turn an ugly situation into a tragic and disastrous one. Explosions of violence, when they came, were not confined to small areas; self-ignited they swept like wildfire through whole sections of the colonial frontier.[59] Neither the British home government nor a combination of the colonies could prevent the self-propelled holocaust from devouring whole Indian societies. The violent forces within the Indian world and the malevolence of the supposedly civilized whites (who nevertheless murdered for scalp bounties) brought about convulsions that continued well into the national period. Uncontrolled passions—greed, hate, fear, and anger—erupting into a whole series of Indian wars, must be assigned some responsibility for what the Cherokees have called the long trail of tears. The colonials, certain of the superiority of the white race and supported by the knowledge of their own power, pushed the Indians aside and took possession of the coastal lands and then occupied the hinterlands of the new continent. The British, unlike their rivals, the French and Spaniards, never developed an overall eighteenth-century colonial policy that gave the Indian a place and a future in the structure of empire.

Over the years we have created and accepted as true our own version of early American Indian history. We have been all too inclined to glorify our ancestors, to portray them as heroic frontiersmen who conquered the wilderness and subdued the wild natives, thus setting the foundations of a new republic. This tendency in American history owes much to the frontier thesis of Frederick Jackson Turner who tended to ignore minority groups, especially the Indians.[60] But we can no longer afford to be satisfied with a version of our history designed primarily to obscure the more dubious actions of our ancestors. There is a need to reexamine the Indian side of our colonial history. The need is pressing and the reassessment of the evidence has already begun. Some of our best scholars (and the Indians themselves) are helping to piece together a more accurate account of what took place. In this new history a central theme will undoubtedly be the persistent struggle of the Indian to preserve his lands and way of life.

NOTES

1– Comment by Bernard Fontana of the University of New Mexico. American Indian History Conference, U.C.L.A., Opening Session, "Opportunities in the Study of Indian History," John W. Caughey, moderator (typescript copy of taped proceedings, May 12, 1967, in the possession of Wilbur R. Jacobs); John W. Caughey, ed., *Opportunities in American Indian Study* (Los Angeles, 1967).

2– Comment by Wilcomb E. Washburn.

3– "Indeitsy" [Indians], *Bol'shaia Sovetskaia Entsiklopediia*, 51 vols. (Moscow, 1949-58), 17:630.

4– Wilbur R. Jacobs and Edmond E. Masson, "History and Propaganda: Soviet Image of the American Past," *Mid-America* (April 1964), 46:75-91.

5– Maurice Marc Wasserman, "The American Indian as Seen by the Seventeenth-Century Chroniclers" (Ph.D. diss., University of Pennsylvania, 1954), pp. 2, 4, 9, 407, 408, 409, 415. See also two well-documented essays: Wilcomb E. Washburn, "The Moral and Legal Justifications for Dispossessing the Indians," and Nancy Oestreich Lurie, "Indian Cultural Adjustment to European Civilization," in James Morton Smith, ed., *Seventeenth-Century America, Essays in Colonial History* (Chapel Hill, N.C., 1959), pp. 15-32, 33-60.

6– Wilbur R. Jacobs, *Wilderness Politics and Indian Gifts, The Northern Colonial Frontier, 1748-1763* (Lincoln, Neb., 1966), pp. 90-114.

7– M. Eugene Sirmans, *Colonial South Carolina, A Political History, 1663-1763* (Chapel Hill, N.C., 1966), pp. 17, 23, 40-43, 53-54, 60; Verner W. Crane, *The Southern Frontier, 1670-1732* (Ann Arbor, Mich., 1964), pp. 19, 31, 80-81, 112-14.

8– Jacobs, *Wilderness Politics*, pp. 148, 165; Wilbur R. Jacobs, ed., *The Appalachian Indian Frontier, The Edmond Atkin Report and Plan of 1755* (Lincoln, Neb., 1967), pp. xvi ff.

9– Jacobs, *Wilderness Politics*, pp. 184-85; Howard H. Peckham, *Pontiac and the Indian Uprising* (Princeton, N.J., 1947), pp. 92-93.

10– A.T. Volwiler, ed., "William Trent's Journal at Fort Pitt, 1763," *Mississippi Valley Historical Review* (December 1924), 11:400. Colonel Henry Bouquet to Amherst, July 13, 1763, contains Colonel Bouquet's answer to Amherst's request, Sylvester K. Stevens and Donald H. Kent, eds., *The Papers of Col. Henry Bouquet*, Pennsylvania State Historical Commission, Series 21634, mimeographed, 19 vols. (Harrisburg, Pa., 1940-43), pp. 214-15.

11– Wilbur R. Jacobs, "The Indian Frontier of 1763," *Western Pennsylvania Historical Magazine* (September 1951), 34:314-22. Louis De Vorsey, Jr., *The Indian Boundary in the Southern Colonies, 1763-1775* (Chapel Hill, N.C., 1966), pp. 27 ff., 48 ff., 93 ff.; William Brandon, *The American Heritage Book of Indians* (New York, 1961), pp. 199-202.

12– William Christie Macleod, *The American Indian Frontier* (New York, 1928), pp. 422-23; Francis Paul Prucha, *American Indian Policy in the Forma-*

tive Years, The Indian Trade and Intercourse Acts, 1790-1834 (Cambridge, Mass., 1962), pp. 3, 26-40, 143 ff.; David H. Corkran, *The Creek Frontier, 1540-1783* (Norman, Okla., 1967), pp. 309-25. Alvin M. Josephy, Jr., *The Indian Heritage of America* (New York, 1968), pp. 314-16. Reginald Horsman's provocative volume, *Expansion and American Indian Policy, 1783-1812* (East Lansing, Mich., 1967), develops the startling thesis that a policy of bringing civilization to the benighted Indian evolved in the first years of the republic because the founding fathers decided that the alternative of exterminating the Indian would probably besmirch the national honor. An excellent appraisal of writings on early American Indian history is Bernard W. Sheehan's "Indian-White Relations in Early America, A Review Essay," *William and Mary Quarterly* (April, 1969), 36:267-86. One of the most valuable essays ever written on Indian behavior is William Fenton's "Factionalism in American Indian Society," *Tirage à part: Actes du IVe Congrès International des Sciences Anthropologiques et Ethnologiques* (Vienna, 1952), Tome II: 330-40.

13— Lurie, "Indian Cultural Adjustment," in *Seventeenth-Century America*, p. 39. Lurie stresses that the specific points which made the European feel superior had little meaning for the seventeenth-century Indians.

14— Wasserman, "The American Indian," pp. 2, 3, 4, 210, 406; William Brandon, "American Indians and American History," *The American West* (Spring 1965), 2:91. In a brilliant article, English literature professor, N. Scott Momaday, a modern scholar of Kiowa Indian ancestry, analyzes Puritan aggressiveness toward the Pequots and the resulting interpretations of the Pequot War. See Momaday, "The Morality of Indian Hating," *Ramparts* (Summer 1964), 3:29-40. An apologist for the Puritans in their early wars is Alden T. Vaughan. See his *New England Frontier, Puritans and Indians, 1620-1675* (Boston, 1965), pp. 134, 309 ff., a work that greatly contrasts with Douglas E. Leach's scholarly and judicious volumes, *Flintlock and Tomahawk, New England in King Philip's War* (New York, 1958), pp. 50 ff., and Leach's *The Northern Colonial Frontier, 1607-1763* (New York, 1966), pp. 36-37, 55-61.

15— For a discussion of Parkman's views on the Indian, see Wilbur R. Jacobs, "Some Social Ideas of Francis Parkman," *The American Quarterly* (Winter 1957), 9:387-96.

16— Washburn, "The Moral and Legal Justifications," in *Seventeenth-Century America*, p. 20. Washburn stresses the modern interpretation of colonial history, envisioning the English invasion of the North American continent as a kind of military beachhead against hostile Indians (ibid., p. 19).

17— Ibid., p. 20. Washburn quotes Alexander Brown, *The First Republic of America* (Boston, 1898), pp. 41-42.

18— Washburn, "The Moral and Legal Justifications," in *Seventeenth-Century America*, p. 19. Washburn cites Roger Clap's "Memoirs" [London, 1731], in Alexander Young, ed., *Chronicles of the First Planters of the Colony of Massachusetts, From 1623 to 1636* (Boston, 1846), p. 350. See also Wasserman, "The American Indian," pp. 3-4 ff.

19– James Adair, *History of the American Indians* (London, 1775), is largely an extended essay comparing the Indians and the ten lost tribes. This theory had been a favorite of European writers. See Lee Eldridge Huddleston, *Origins of the American Indians, European Concepts, 1492-1729* (Austin, Texas, 1967), pp. 33-47.

20– *Minutes of the Provincial Council of Pennsylvania* (Philadelphia, 1852), 9:138-42, contains the complete text of the "Remonstrance" made by the Paxton rioters. Franklin, in an unsigned pamphlet, criticized the rioters for murdering peaceful natives: "The only Crime of these poor Wretches seems to have been that they had reddish brown Skin, and black hair" (*A Narrative of the Late Massacres, in Lancaster County, of a Number of Indians* ... [Philadelphia, 1764]). See also Wilbur R. Jacobs, ed., *The Paxton Riots and the Frontier Theory* (Chicago, 1967), pp. 8-29.

21– An interesting discussion of this question appears in Bernard W. Sheehan, "Civilization and the American Indian in the Thought of the Jeffersonian Era," (Ph.D. diss., University of Virginia, 1965), pp. 251 ff. Sheehan, in tracing the origins of European attitudes toward the land, points out that John Locke, in his *Second Treatise on Civil Government*, associated ownership of property with cultivation. Theodore Roosevelt later referred to Indian lands as a "game preserve" (ibid.) See Georgiana C. Nammack, "A Century of Conflict: Politics and Rivalries Over Indian Lands in Colonial New York," (Ph.D. diss., University of California, Santa Barbara, 1963), pp. 1-9, for an excellent discussion on European and Indian concepts of land ownership. Washburn, "The Moral and Legal Justifications," in *Seventeenth-Century America*, pp. 23 ff., also deals with the historic background of conflicting Indian-white claims to the land.

22– Lurie, "Indian Cultural Adjustment," in *Seventeenth-Century America*, pp. 39-40.

23– Jacobs, *Wilderness Politics*, pp. 42, 59, 73; Huntington Library Collection of Loudoun Papers, nos. 3517, 3246, contain Superintendent Edmond Atkin's comments on equipment used by smiths.

24– References to Indian generosity and kindness are detailed in Brandon, "American Indians and American History," p. 17, and in Washburn, "The Moral and Legal Justifications," in *Seventeenth-Century America*, pp. 19 ff. Edmund S. Morgan, quoting the writings of surveyor John Lawson of North Carolina, points out that Indian notions of hospitality were so generous that a white visitor was often provided with one of the attractive maidens of the tribe, and the children of the couple usually were raised as Indians. Edmund S. Morgan, "The American Indian: Incorrigible Individualist," *Mirror of the Indian* (Booklet published by the Associates of the John Carter Brown Library, Providence, R.I., 1958), p. 10.

25– Brandon, "American Indians and American History," p. 25, quoting Robert Rogers, *A Concise Account of North America* (London, 1765).

26– Johnson to Arthur Lee, February 28, 1771, E.B. O'Callaghan, ed., *Documentary History of the State of New York* (New York, 1851), 4:430-39.

27– Ibid. See also Wilbur R. Jacobs, "Unsavory Sidelights on the Colonial Fur Trade," *New York History* (April 1953), 34:135-48.

28– Lee to Miss Sidney Lee, June 18, 1756, *Collections of the New-York Historical Society for the Year 1871* (New York, 1872), 1:3.

29– Ibid.

30– Jacobs, ed., *The Appalachian Indian Frontier*, p. 68.

31– Ibid., p. 38.

32– Roy Harvey Pearce, writing in his influential volume, *The Savages of America*, in a chapter entitled "An Impassable Gulf: The Social and Historical Image," puts the question in this fashion: "The discovery of America furnished savages in abundance. The question was: How noble were they? . . . the forces which informed the idea of savagism at one and the same time destroyed the idea of the noble savage and made isolated radicals of those who would believe in it" (*The Savages of America, A Study of the Indian and the Idea of Civilization*, rev. ed. [Baltimore, 1965], p. 136). Bernard W. Sheehan, in a chapter on "Violence," concludes that "the Indian's penchant for the most exotic brands of violence . . . commanded a realistic appraisal of his savage character" ("Civilization and the Indian," p. 325).

33– Governor Alexander Spotswood of Virginia in a long letter to the Board of Trade, April 5, 1717, R.A. Brock, ed., *The Official Letters of Alexander Spotswood* (Richmond, Va., 1885), 2:227, comments on this point.

34– Sheehan, "Civilization and the Indian," pp. 140 ff.; Prucha, *American Indian Policy*, pp. 215, 217; William T. Hagan, *American Indians* (Chicago, 1961), p. 54.

35– William C. Reichel, ed., *Memorials of the Moravian Church* (Philadelphia, 1870), 1:95-96.

36– Francis Parkman, *The Conspiracy of Pontiac and the Indian War After the Conquest of Canada* (Boston, 1899), 2:246-49.

37– Macleod, *The American Indian Frontier*, pp. 359-60.

38– Spotswood to the Board of Trade, April 5, 1717, in *The Official Letters of Alexander Spotswood*, 2:227.

39– "CONSIDERATIONS For Securing, Improving & Enlarging your Majesty's Dominions in America," September 8, 1721, E.B. O'Callaghan et al., eds., *Documents Relative to the Colonial History of New York* (Albany, 1855), 5:627.

40– Jacobs, *Wilderness Politics*, p. 170. Governor Robert H. Morris declared war on the Delawares on April 14, 1756 (*Minutes of the Provincial Council of Pennsylvania*[Philadelphia, 1852], 7:88).

41– Jacobs, ed., *The Appalachian Indian Frontier*, p. 40.

42– George Edward Reed, ed., *Pennsylvania Archives*, 4th series (Harrisburg, Pa., 1900), 3:292-93; Jacobs, ed., *The Paxton Riots*, pp. 33-34.

43— Atkin to Horatio Sharpe, June 30, 1757, Samuel Hazard, ed., *Pennsylvania Archives*, 1st series (Philadelphia, 1852), 3:199.

44— Jacobs, *Wilderness Politics*, pp. 138-39, n.

45— John Fitzpatrick, ed., *The Writings of George Washington* . . . (Washington, D.C., 1931), 1:97, 115.

46— See Douglas E. Leach's free transcription of the treaty in his edition of *A Rhode Islander Reports on King Philip's War, The Second Harris Letter of August, 1676* (Providence, R.I., 1963), pp. 89-95.

47— Ibid., pp. 6-7. Douglas Leach suggests that the attack was based upon "the theory of preventive war and . . . the potential market value of Narragansett land . . . . (*The Northern Colonial Frontier, 1607-1763*, pp. 66-67). In his earlier work, *Flintlock and Tomahawk*, Professor Leach stresses the Narragansett's treachery as a justification for the Massachusetts' attack (pp. 112 ff.).

48— "Treaty of Logg's Town," *Virginia Magazine of History and Biography* (October 1905), 13:154-74.

49— "Indian Proceedings at Mount Johnson," June 17-21, 1755, James Sullivan et al., eds., *The Papers of Sir William Johnson* (New York, 1921), 1:640-42.

50— For a partial list of other important Indian treaties of the colonial era, see Henry F. DePuy, *A Bibliography of English Colonial Treaties with the American Indians Including a Synopsis of Each Treaty* (New York, 1917). A number of significant treaties are discussed by the editors in their introduction in Carl Van Doren and Julian P. Boyd, eds., *Indian Treaties Printed by Benjamin Franklin, 1736-1762: Their Literary, Historical, and Bibliographical Significance* (Philadelphia, 1938).

51— Crane, *The Southern Frontier, 1670-1732*, pp. 80 ff. A description of the Carolina Indian slave trade appears in Sirmans, *Colonial South Carolina*, pp. 33, 38, 40-43, 47, 53-54, 60.

52— Yasuhide Kawashima, "Indians and the Law in Colonial Massachusetts, 1689-1763" (Ph.D. diss., University of California, Santa Barbara, 1967), pp. 28, 281. In 1712 Massachusetts passed an act "prohibiting the Importation or Bringing into this Province . . . Indian Servants or Slaves." Ibid., p. 282.

53— Ibid., pp. 280 ff. See also Winthrop D. Jordan, *White Over Black, American Attitudes Toward the Negro, 1550-1812* (Chapel Hill, N.C., 1968), pp. 66-69, for a brief discussion of enslavement of Indians in New England.

54— Crane, *The Southern Frontier, 1670-1732*, pp. 80 ff.

55— Ibid., pp. 112-14.

56— Robert Rogers, *Ponteach: or the Savages of America, A Tragedy* (London, 1766), pp. 3-5.

57— Frank J. Klingberg, *Anglican Humanitarianism in Colonial New York* (Philadelphia, 1940), pp. 79-81; Jacobs, *Wilderness Politics*, pp. 33, 34, 107.

58— Nammack, "A Century of Conflict," pp. 103-108.

59– Brandon, *The American Heritage Book of Indians*, pp. 187-202, includes an excellent analysis of Indian-White conflict in the colonial era. See also Macleod, *The American Indian Frontier*, pp. 209-292.

60– Turner, in his well-known essay, "The Significance of the Frontier in American History," dismissed the Indian as "a consolidating agent" helping to bring about intercolonial cooperation for defense (*The Frontier in American History* [New York, 1921], p. 15). This theme is echoed in Turner's lectures: "The Indians had step by step, in successive wars, . . . influenced white development by this retardation of advance, compelling society to organize & consolidate in order to hold the frontier; training it in military discipline; determining the rate of advance, particularly at the points where the mt. barriers broke down . . ." (quoted from Turner's notes summarizing a semester's lectures on the West at Harvard, about 1921, TU File Drawer 13, Turner Papers, Huntington Library. I am indebted to Ray Billington and William Brandon for calling my attention to this manuscript). Parts of Turner's notes are also quoted in Brandon, "American Indians and American History," pp. 14-15, where Brandon makes the point that American historians have tended to regard Indians as natural features of the land or as troublesome "wild varmints" (p. 14). A recent example of whitewashing the history of American Indian-white relations is the pamphlet, *The American Indian, Questions and Answers*, U.S. Information Service, 2nd ed. (Washington, 1968). On page 6 of this attractively illustrated booklet one finds, for instance, the statement that the federal government "has negotiated some 370 treaties and enacted thousands of laws on their [the Indians'] behalf." Nowhere in this booklet, aside from the statement that Indians were victimized by traders, is there an accurate summary of the history of federal Indian policy.

Political Incorporation and Cultural Change in New Spain: A Study in Spanish-Indian Relations

Edward H. Spicer

As a result of the military conquest of mainland America in the 1520s, Spain was faced with the problem of incorporating a very large population of non-European cultural background into her political system. One immediate effect was an ideological conflict among Spaniards which continued for three-quarters of a century, coming to a focus during its last phase in the Las Casas-Sepúlveda controversy.[1] The conflict centered on rival conceptions of social justice in the relations between Spaniards and the inhabitants of the New World. Specifically, Spaniards split over the issues of what was a just war against Indians, what was a just basis for title to land, and what were the right techniques for bringing Indians to accept the Spanish variety of civilization. The controversy may be seen as an effort to examine the ethical assumptions on which relations between Spaniards and Indians might be developed. This involved bringing into a consistent, logical relationship divergent views of the fundamental nature of non-Christians and of the place in the universe of non-Christians in relation to Spaniards. Aristotelian ethics and social concepts, the Christian ideology of divine purpose, and the Spaniards' views of their working social universe all had to be harmonized. The outcome of this process of intellectual and moral reorientation was the attainment of a new level of ideological inte-

gration. It required many years and the expenditure of great energy
in oral debate and writing. Some of the results were quite concrete,
such as written statements like the Laws of Burgos and the New
Laws of the Indies. Codification of the results of controversy did
not, of course, mean that Spaniards generally accepted the principles
so formulated. A variety of social and economic influences were in
operation at the level of face to face contacts. It became quite clear
that policy was one thing and practice was another. Ideological and
sociopolitical integration were distinct, although mutually influenc-
ing, processes. The kind of dominance which the Spanish-derived
cultural system achieved during three hundred years was a product
of these and, of course, other cultural processes.

In what follows we shall focus on processes of sociopolitical
integration, examining these from two points of view: (1) The kind
of integration between Spanish and Indian communities which came
about during the colonial period, and (2) The effects of the integra-
tive processes on the Indian societies. The description here does not
pretend to be exhaustive for New Spain, but is limited to a selection
of cases where there is some indication that they broadly represent
the range of variation. Whether or not they do encompass the whole
range remains to be demonstrated through further analysis along the
lines undertaken here.

Our attention will be directed to what took place in four areas
of New Spain where notably different kinds of relations between
Spaniards and Indians developed. One of these is the Valley of
Mexico where the Indians were descendants of the Aztecs. A second
area is northwestern Mexico where the Yaqui and Mayo Indians lived
in what is now Sonora and Sinaloa. The third includes a portion of
the extreme northern extension of New Spain in the present state of
New Mexico where so-called Pueblo Indians constituted a major part
of the population. The fourth area is western Mexico, embracing the
Bajío, where many Indians were of Tarascan cultural background.

In these four areas the Indian societies, at the time of the
Spanish invasions, were of quite different types. In certain important but not decisive ways, these cultural differences influenced the
course of integration. More fundamental in influence were the needs

of the Spaniards as they faced the different ecological and demographic situations. The variety of processes which these and other cases exhibit is indicative of the wide adaptive potential of the Spanish social system. The nature of its complexity and of its essential integrating mechanisms becomes a little clearer in the light of a better understanding of the variety of contact communities which Spaniards established.

AZTEC INCORPORATION

It has often been said that Aztec society was decapitated by the Spaniards. This metaphor is frequently used further with the implication that the Spaniards found it easy to integrate the Aztecs into their political system by merely placing a new head on the body of the Indian society. It was necessary, so it is implied, only to replace the upper levels of the politico-ecclesiastical hierarchy and put in their place either Spaniards or retrained Aztec nobility. The metaphor—decapitation and subsequent "re-capitation"—interpreted in this way is extremely misleading. There can, of course, be no question about the widespread substitution of Spaniards or reoriented Aztecs for former top administrators. However, this new head made a very different kind of juncture with the old body of Aztec society from what had previously existed. To carry the metaphor further, and perhaps thus to help usher it out of the literature altogether, the new juncture healed over in such a way that the circulation between body and head was very seriously impeded and masses of scar tissue formed which increasingly, over three hundred years, interfered with the articulation of the head and the shoulders.

The detailed studies of Professor Gibson have added greatly to our understanding of the processes of political incorporation among the Aztecs of the Valley of Mexico.[2] I shall rely heavily on his findings and, in fact, do little beyond giving some different emphases by way of relating his data to the theme of this paper. It is quite clear that what happened in the Valley of Mexico between 1520 and 1820 was a progressive alienation and disarticulation of Indian political life from that of the Spaniards and mestizos. This was not the aim of Spanish policy. However, one objective was to protect Indian society from disruption. The pursuit of this objective was one of the results of the ideological conflict and was an indication of royal acceptance of one of the major propositions of Las Casas—namely, that Indians had achieved a degree of political organization and that Spaniards consequently had no just mandate to usurp power completely in Indian communities. Action in accord with this principle led to a kind of protective separation of Spaniards, Negroes, and mestizos from Indians. Regulations were formulated which restricted Spaniards from taking up residence in Indian communities and which defined required distances between Indian and non-Indian towns and their lands. The Spaniards also introduced a blueprint for organization of local government in Indian communities designed to give Indians a high degree of autonomy in local affairs, as in rural Spain. Along with this went the establishment of a system of Indian courts specially designed to administer justice within the Indian social world. These measures certainly stemmed in part from the influence of Las Casas, but they were also consistent with recognition of the fact that in the West Indies the encomienda system had wiped out a major economic resource, namely, the Indian population itself. This population as a tribute-paying people was an important asset of the crown. Thus both economic and ideological interests were served by a program of nondisruption of Indian society. However, as executed it did not result in the persistence of Indian society in the form which it had at the arrival of the Spaniards. The policy of protection or preservation of the Indian social order was consistent neither with the missionary aim of transforming the moral order nor with the royal objective of a constant flow of tribute.

The political structure of corregimiento became the dominant political system after about 1570 in the Valley of Mexico. This system could hardly have been better designed to inhibit the growth of the concept or encouragement of the role of "free citizen of Spain." At point after point, the political organization discouraged Indian participation in local government and prevented the growth of a sense of responsibility upward from the lower political levels. The heart of the matter was the basically exploitative character of the whole political system of New Spain. It neither encouraged the development of a new type of more inclusive political organization, nor allowed the Aztec forms of organization to persist even at the local level. A Spanish system of political roles was indeed imposed with the necessary corresponding Indian roles, but motivations for performing in these roles were not generated within Indian society and there was no merging of political or supporting values through the operation of the system. There was, on the contrary, the stimulation of a division of interests with consequent differentiation of political orientations and organization. Even by the middle of the seventeenth century, a process of withdrawal of the Indians into their own political life was under way.

To Spanish officials of various kinds, most notably the ecclesiastics, the Indians had come, by the end of the 1700s, to be regarded as a race apart—not only fundamentally different in customs, but also distinct in goals and basic morality from the Spaniards and Creoles. The negative concept of Indians which Las Casas had worked so industriously to forestall had become generally accepted among the Spaniards of New Spain. The very system of social relations which Las Casas' views had in large part sanctioned produced distinct cultural worlds which stimulated the views he regarded as wrong. The cultural world of the descendants of the Aztecs did not become an integral part of the Spanish Christian world, nor did it remain Aztec.

How did this situation come about? The facts seem fairly well established but stand in need of some interpretation in processual terms. The institutional linkage of the Aztecs in the Valley of Mexico, which was of major importance throughout the colonial period, was the corregimiento organization. The encomienda played some early part in a kind of decentralizing of the Aztec political system, the incorporating of *tlatoani* (Aztec upper-class families) into the Spanish political organization, and the disrupting of the basis of local government. To this extent the encomiendas laid some foundations for later developments. However, the encomienda system became steadily of less and less influence on Aztec life after 1570, by which time all the large encomiendas had been eliminated.

In the late 1700s there was the beginning of modification of the political structure through the intendancy organization, but this hardly took hold. The major instrument of political incorporation was the corregimiento during nearly the whole of the three-hundred-year period under consideration. Understanding the nature of this network of roles leads to a grasp of the character of the processes of political incorporation which came into operation. The missionaries operated as beneficiaries of, and auxiliaries to, the corregimiento system. We may therefore treat the ecclesiastical organization as a part of the system of the corregidors, especially after secularization.

The operation of the encomiendas brought about conditions which could not be sanctioned in the ideology crystalized during the Las Casas controversy. Further, the encomienda system was a serious threat to the power of the crown. The corregimiento system was established as the mechanism for insuring crown control of and direct benefit from Indian labor and tribute, and for bringing Indian communities, with the aid of the ecclesiastics, into the empire as fully functioning local governments and cultural units. The explicit aim was incorporation of Indians as citizens with a minimum of disruption of their society. The foundation was not to be the destruction of Indian community organization, but its reorganization as political and ecclesiastical units, after the Spanish fashion, with a considerable measure of local autonomy. The roles appropriate to villages and parishes in Spain were introduced and Indians selected to fill them. Key roles in the linkage with the wider network beyond the local level were those of corregidor, missionary, and governor—the first two filled by Spaniards or Creoles, the last by Indians.

The office of corregidor was well designed to carry out the interests of the Spanish crown in maintaining a colonial administration which would insure a flow of surpluses from the colony. The corregidor was appointed and his salary set by the viceroy. He operated at no expense to the colonial administration, however, since his salary was derived from his collections from the Indians. The whole expense of administration was carried by the Indian communities. These expenses were, of course, covered by tribute, and a major function of the corregidor was the collection of tribute. All that was collected flowed out of the Indian communities, except what went for the support of the ecclesiastics. The expenses of local administration and the labor for public works had to be raised apart from the tribute funds by the Indians. In addition, the corregidor was responsible for recruiting the labor pools required for general public works, such as flood control in the Valley of Mexico. The corregidor was thus the representative of outside interests. It is impossible to interpret anyone in this position as having any concern for local needs and problems. The local communities had no controls whatever over the corregidor, and hence he habitually collected what the traffic would bear. This led, in irregular fashion, as Gibson and others have well pointed out, to officially unauthorized collections—the *derramas*.[3] The corregidor was, of course, subject to supervision and review from above, but this merely limited the range of his exploitive activities and did not alter the basic character of the system.

To some extent, as we have indicated, there was a little channeling of tribute and the products of Indian labor back into the communities through the ecclesiastical organization. Whatever came back in this form was, however, determined beyond the local level, and, in this sense, was seen by the Indians in the same light as they saw the activity of the corregidors. In contrast with the corregidors, the missionaries lived in close contact with the Indians and this made some difference. There was, indeed, some identification by Indians of their interests with those of the missionaries and some support of the ecclesiastics vis-à-vis civil authorities. But, as some accounts indicate, there was decreasing contact of this sort as church functionaries concentrated in Mexico City, and, late in the colonial period, there was often only one priest for every three thousand Indian families. As secularization proceeded in the eighteenth century, there was less and less tendency for any common cause to develop between Indians and ecclesiastics. The ecclesiastical linkage declined as an integral part of community life and became in fact more and more indistinguishable from the corregimiento control.

The local organization, which the Spaniards introduced as the base of civil and church structure, was modeled along lines of existing rural institutions in Spain, but with influences from the ancient blueprints of imperial Rome. Its nucleus was an annually elected set of officers with a governor as top official. However, in a basic sense this institution was not only designed but was also taken over by the corregimiento. The election of each *cabecera* village was rather carefully supervised by the corregidor himself. He had orders to be present at elections of governors and also instructions to see that "Christian Indians" were chosen for the office. The governor was inextricably linked with the corregidor, for his basic duties consisted in the actual collection of tribute, for which the corregidor had responsibility to the viceroy, and the recruiting and organization of the labor gangs under the direction of the corregidor. Other duties—such as the maintenance of law and order—were shared with the Spanish alcaldes and *alguaciles* of the corregimiento organization.

Thus the governor was primarily an instrument of indirect rule and of communication in connection with the fulfillment of the demands of the colonial administration. Under these circumstances it became increasingly difficult by the last half of the 1700s to get Indians to serve as governors. It is easy to see why in the light of an understanding of the inherent nature of the role. Major responsibilities were clearly defined upward for maintaining the tribute system, and no real opportunity for serving local needs in an important way was open. Individual governors here and there might use their offices for personal gain as they became willing parts of the Spanish political system, but even such use of the office was inhibited by the short tenure. Moreover, the corregimiento was modified during the eighteenth century in directions which steadily decreased the possibilities not only for relating the job to community interests, but also for turning it to personal account.

As the overall Spanish political system rigidified, it became less responsive to the economic developments in New Spain. This resulted in a steady increase in the amount of tribute demanded, and the governors were required to become personally liable for any arrears of their communities. In addition, probably in response to the declining effectiveness of the local government, there was increasing outside control of the funds in the *caja de comunidad* raised for local use. These circumstances led to declining motivation for participation in local government. A sure indicator of what was happening was to be found in the loss of interest in maintaining and renewing public buildings and community facilities. By about 1800, the Spanish program had led to the creation of a shell of political organization in which Indians were participating less and less.

Under this system the Indians did not, of course, cease to exist as some kind of human community. The people continued to live on pretty much the traditional, if often considerably contracted, locations. And people do not exist without some sort of organization. But the structure of their groupings had profoundly changed. During the early phase when most of the Indians in the Valley of Mexico were living under the control of *encomenderos*, there had been a short period when it appeared that the Aztec class structure might be integrated into the Spanish social system. The *tlatoani* often became the connecting links with the *encomendero* and his representatives. However, the Spanish social system, as it developed in New Spain, did not provide a place for the former upper class except by absorption. A gradual leveling in the Indian communities took place so that the native class system did not survive after the corregimiento system became dominant. The whole basis of authority within the Indian communities was in process of alteration. The class structure was breaking down as *tlatoani* became absorbed into Creole society or failed to maintain position under the new circumstances. The priestly class was eliminated and replaced, for a time, by the increasingly influential missionaries. The Aztec formal educational system, which had been a major support for the class system, ceased to function as it was discouraged by the missionaries; schools were established outside the communities for "sons of caciques" exclusively. As Gibson has pointed out, a general feeling of new freedom pervaded many communities.[4] At the same time, throughout the sixteenth and on into the seventeenth century, population decline was drastic and contributed to the disruption of the old order. It was during this period of dislocation that the corregimiento system took hold. For a hundred years or more it appeared that the locally introduced politico-ecclesiastical organization might succeed and bring the Aztec communities in as participating units in the Spanish system. The Indians had begun to make use of the court system set up exclusively for their benefit, and they uniformly established town governments according to Spanish prescription. However, as we have seen, the institutional means were not adaptable to bringing about the sort of integration which Las Casas might have envisioned, and the trend of community development took another direction, especially after the mid 1600s.

The ecological situation had now shifted greatly. The increase in population, coupled with the establishment of the hacienda as a new institution competing for land, labor, and loyalty, was a factor in the stimulation of the two new processes which began to affect Indian society during the final century of the colonial period. On the one hand there was the process of reorientation of Indian life toward the hacienda and its advantages. At first wages were increasing, and they offered a kind of economic security. Indians in some numbers moved into the new situation, were oriented away from the Indian communities, and ceased to identify with them. On the other hand, the population of the Indian communities in the Valley of Mexico was not declining, despite the drain of people to the haciendas. The increasing population of the Indian towns influenced the other dominant process.

This process we might call the disengagement of the Indian communities from involvement in the Spanish social system—political and cultural. So far we have discussed this in terms of the withdrawal from participation in the political organization which had linked the Indian communities with the Spanish society. We must supplement this with consideration of what the Indian communities were becoming internally.

Each Indian community became a different kind of social and cultural entity from what it had been either under the Aztec system or the first phase of the colonial situation. The fluid condition in the social structure, which had characterized the Aztec communities during the preceding century and a half, began to alter. One among the various possibilities for reorientation and reorganization was accepted. In general the major influence was the intensification of the exploitive nature of the Spanish system. The Indian communities responded to this trend by themselves becoming more tightly integrated and rigidly oriented away from participation in Spanish society.

There were other causes. For one thing the land base of the community was not what it had been before. In most instances it had been reduced. Where this had not taken place, it was more and more certain that the threat of the haciendas and Spanish landholders was increasing. Many Indian communities were checkerboarded with land which had, under one stress or another, been rented to Spaniards or Creoles. The sense of a contracting land base was also intensified by the steadily increasing populations of many Indian communities, despite losses of population to the hacienda labor forces. At the same time basic well-being on what land was left under local control was threatened as the tribute collections became greater and communities found themselves in arrears. Under these conditions nonparticipation in the Spanish political system became a dominating value—a symbolic defense, at least, against the exploitation of which it was the means. Withdrawal from the dominant society, and defense against its institutionalized efforts to appropriate land and income, became the foundations of relations with Spaniards and mestizos.

The contracted local community became the total sphere of social and expressive life. It was not an Aztec community culturally because Aztec local organization, whether ceremonial or political, had been effectively disrupted. The Indian religious hierarchy, the Aztec class structure, and the local *calpulli* organization of education, military, and political institutions, had ceased to operate almost within a decade after Spanish domination. Moreover, not only had these forms for ordered social life been disrupted, but also the Spanish agents of change—chiefly the ecclesiastics—were busily introducing new forms: the political structure of the Indian pueblo with its governor and his assistants, the church organization below the level of the missionary or priest; the barrio, the chapel, and the *cofradía* organization. These forms were introduced into disintegrating communities. They were imposed, but also they were voluntarily accepted. They served the purposes of the missionaries and Spanish civil authorities, and they came eventually to serve some of the purposes of the local people.

Continuing experience demonstrated that the welfare of the local community was not positively related to the corregidor and his link with the outside-sanctioned local government, the *gobernador*. There were few, if any, benefits connected with this linkage, but rather losses and disadvantages in the form of tribute payments, labor levies, and other interferences in local affairs. The areas of collective effort farthest removed from the corregidor network became the foci of local interest. These were the institutions of the barrios (in the larger, *cabecera* towns) and the non-*cabecera* local communities. The *mayordomo* organizations of the barrio and *aldea* chapels became one focus of purely Indian activities. The other consisted of those *cofradía* organizations which included only Indians.[5] Community welfare came to be regarded as being bound up with the saints of these social units. In large part, of course, these supernatural guardians of the welfare were perhaps what they had been formerly, but with new names as Christian saints and with somewhat modified cult organization, deeply influenced by the *cofradía* system introduced by the missionaries. Collective labor, in the interest of the Indians, was organized in terms of these subunits of the *cabecera* both for public works and for maintenance of the working relations with the supernaturals. There came to be a purely Indian-managed area of community organization, and this was characterized by a lower level of integration than had characterized the Aztec communities.

The various *mayordomo* organizations were nevertheless in some degree coordinated at the level of the *cabeceras*. This was accomplished through the principales, or elders, whose authority derived not from the corregidor, but from the conduct of their lives in the world of Indian values and sanctions. The operations of the elders remained somewhat mysterious to the Spanish officials. They were sometimes correctly diagnosed by the latter as subversive with respect to the purposes of the corregidor system, for the elders focused on maintaining a buffer organization to keep, insofar as possible, the corregidor-governor arrangement at arm's length. As the lands of the community contracted and continued to be attacked, the social life of the community also contracted. Under the guidance of the elders, it developed a fiercely defensive orientation in the narrow sphere of community or barrio life. The politico-ecclesiastical system of organization of the Spaniards had brought about the acceptance of neither the universalistic orientation of Christianity, nor the higher level of integration of the Spanish state.

YAQUI INCORPORATION

To assume that the processes set in motion in the heartland were universal in New Spain is to lay a foundation for misunderstanding not only the nature of the Spanish colonial system, but also the problems of the Mexican political structure which arose out of the ruins of New Spain. There were other modes of political incorporation with quite diverse effects on the Indian societies.

The military conquest of most of the northwest of New Spain proceeded differently from that in the central part. A separate campaign was required for each tribal group, and Spanish control was instituted almost tribe by tribe, or subtribe by subtribe. Moreover, effective control was established relatively late and there were often no missionaries immediately available to begin the religious conquest. The Yaquis were not brought into the Spanish system until 1617, nearly a century after the conquest of the Aztecs, and then only because of the failure of Spanish military campaigns against the Indians.

The process of incorporation was characterized by striking differences compared to what took place among the Aztecs.[6] In the first place, the Yaqui area, and most of northwestern New Spain, was placed in the hands of the Jesuits who worked quite differently from the Franciscans. They entered the Yaqui country without military escort and proceeded to convert by persuasion, along the lines advocated by Las Casas. For a century and a quarter following their entrance in 1617, the Jesuits worked pretty much alone without interference from Spanish military or political authorities. Moreover, Spanish settlers did not become a factor in the Yaqui country during

119

this first phase. The encomieda system was not brought into operation at any time. In effect, the only agency operative in incorporation, until about 1740, was the Jesuit order.

The Jesuits developed, as the incorporating institution, the mission community, which bore only superficial resemblance to the *cabecera-sujeto* political structure of central New Spain. The mission community was a political entity organized in terms of the offices of Spanish local government, but not channeling tribute or labor to the crown. The Jesuit missionaries and their staffs effected the political reorganization of Yaqui communities and maintained their dominance during the first 125 years. The resident missionary controlled the Yaqui towns in the sense that he initially defined, in main outline, the roles of Yaqui officeholders and influenced, in some degree, the selection of officials. But the missionary did not collect tribute for the crown. What was put into effect, however, amounted to something resembling the tribute system. Within a few years after the Jesuit reorganization of the Yaqui settlements, each town was raising a surplus of wheat, corn, and livestock. The grain was stored locally in two of the eight Yaqui towns in newly built warehouses of stone, and the growing herds were maintained on the town lands. The Jesuits were able to persuade Yaquis to work for the creation of this agricultural surplus, a portion of which went for the maintenance of the very small missionary staff in each town. Perhaps the greater part of what was produced was devoted to furthering the missionary program in the northwest. During the 1600s the Yaqui towns became the bases of supply and outfitting for the extension of Jesuit work in lower California and among the Opata and Pima missions to the northwest. Many Yaquis assisted the Jesuits in this growing effort.

Thus there was a system of tribute established by the Jesuits, but the use of the missionary stimulated surplus was turned back into the communities locally to some extent, and Yaquis participated with the Jesuits in its further use outside the Yaqui country. The ways in which their products were being used were largely visible to the Yaquis. Dealings with outsiders were channeled through the missionaries, most of whom maintained residence for extended periods in the Yaqui communities. The relations between Jesuits and Yaquis began as friendly ones, the missionaries having in fact been asked for by the Yaquis. This kind of cooperation continued with little interruption until the 1730s.

By that time a few Spanish settlers had moved up to the edge of the Yaqui country, and the colonial administration, which had its seat several hundred miles to the south, began increasingly to look toward breaking Jesuit control of the mission communities. Friction between civil officials and the missionaries developed and culminated in disturbances in the Yaqui and neighboring Indian towns. A revolt occurred in 1740. This resulted in the first effective assertion of military power over the Yaquis and a temporary elimination of the missionaries. A presidio was established at the edge of Yaqui country and Spanish settlers became more numerous. It was not until 1767, however, that the missionary establishment was much affected. In that year the Jesuits were expelled from the New World, and the Yaqui towns came first under Franciscan management and then were secularized. Through the 1700s tribute collections were not made for various reasons—chief being the fears of provincial officials that tribute collection would lead to Indian uprisings which had been too serious to ignore, as in the 1740 revolt of the Yaquis. Thus throughout the colonial period the Yaquis underwent incorporation in a profoundly different way from the Aztecs, the process taking place through the institution of the mission community, not through encomienda, corregimiento, or hacienda.

The mission community of the northwest was different from Indian towns to the south not only in that it was tribute exempt but, in many cases, little subject to *repartimiento*, taking Indians outside their own communities. It was different not only in that it was not under direct control of the civil administration, but it was different also in internal structure; as a result its development within the Spanish empire took a very different path from the Aztec postconquest town. In the northwestern provinces, with the exception of New Mexico, the mission community was a new concentration of smaller *ranchería* populations grouped around churches built under the direction of missionaries. Among the Yaquis, these were settlements

121

of from two to four thousand, and they maintained such size for the two hundred years of colonial rule. The Yaqui population of twenty-five to thirty thousand was not reduced by disease or other causes during the colonial period.

In the Yaqui mission communities there was a growth and expansion of political life through the whole of the colonial period. In contrast with the process of withdrawal noted for the south there was intensifying participation in the new town organizations. This began under the nominal direction of the missionaries, but it was characterized by the development of voluntary participation. There was no more than one missionary for every five or six hundred families. The result was a politico-ecclesiastical structure in which there was significant role-filling by Yaquis. It was by no means a replica of Spanish local organization any more than it was a persistence of Yaqui forms. The Yaqui town, by the end of the first century of contact with the missionaries, was an emergent form of local government. Its offices were for the most part named by Spanish names, such as *gobernador*, *alguacil*, *capitán*, *sacristán*, *fiscal*, etc. But each of these had its Yaqui form, respectively for those mentioned, *kobanao*, *alawasin*, *kapitan*, *temasti*, *piscan*, etc. Each town was integrated through five systems of authority, or *ya'uram*, as Yaquis called them: the civil, military, church, fiesta or cargo, and customs authorities. Recruitment for office combined the Spanish annual election and the *manda*, a fusion of Christian vow and a form of Indian ceremonial dedication. Each town had several hundred formal officeholders, combining functions of local government, ceremonial management, and military organization. Towns were autonomous entities, although forms of military organization permitted effective unification for war purposes. They also recognized the overall authority of the Jesuit and papal organization and functioned within that international framework. The attempt of the Spanish civil authorities to tie the towns into their tribute-collecting organization about 1740 resulted in temporary disruption, but almost immediately the earlier town integration was vigorously reconstituted.

Thus we see a process almost the opposite of that which was taking place in the Aztec communities. To say that this was a result merely of isolation from the center is to miss the point of what was happening. It was rather a situation in which there was intensive contact with only one segment of the complex Spanish society, chiefly the Jesuit ecclesiastics who were using a framework—the local organization—decreed by the crown, but which was developing in its own way. The religious orientation of Spain was being carried to the Yaquis, but it was being done in a situation in which ecclesiastics and Indians were integrating largely apart from the civil-military arm of the Spanish government, and even with the intrusion of settlers it remained uncomplicated for over a century. Settlers began to influence the development only after a foundation of reoriented Indian communities had evolved. These newly oriented units were strong enough to persist under the new pressures introduced irregularly through the eighteenth century, including the imposition of military control with the establishment of a presidio at the edge of Yaqui country after the 1740 revolt.

The major process was not withdrawal from the dominant political structure, but rather the development of a new form of local organization and the emergence of a new cultural system within the whole. This culture was a product of the interaction of Yaquis with a relatively few Spaniards who introduced a special selection of Spanish cultural elements. Selection and modification by Yaquis was possible with respect to political and military organization, economic orientation, and religious concept and practice. By the beginning of the nineteenth century this emergent Yaqui culture was well established.

INCORPORATION OF THE
PUEBLOS OF NEW MEXICO

A situation like neither that of the Aztecs or the Yaquis developed on the extreme northern border of New Spain. Here the conditions of contact between Spaniards and Indians were in basic ways more similar to that of the Aztecs than the Yaquis, but the native culture was extremely different from the Aztec. The nature of the Pueblo cultural system played an important part in the different re-

123

sults, but there were also profoundly influential features of the contact community.

The military conquest of the Pueblos took place in 1540, within twenty years after that of the Aztecs. However, little was done to institute the process of political incorporation until several thousand Spanish and Tlaxcalan colonists in 1598 settled in the upper Rio Grande Valley. It was not until 1610 that troubles among the colonists were smoothed over and the permanent settlement of Santa Fe was founded. Thus the process of incorporating the Pueblo Indians into the Spanish political system began more or less contemporaneously with that of the Yaquis and other Indians of northwestern New Spain. The two hundred years until the end of the Spanish regime were characterized by two distinct phases in the relations between Spaniards and Indians.[7]

The first phase may be taken to include the period from the founding of the colony at Santa Fe until what has been called the reconquest of the Pueblos beginning in 1692. It was characterized by the introduction of the standard institutions of Spanish dominance, namely, encomienda, *repartimiento* and tribute, corregimiento, missions and ecclesiastical tribunals, the Spanish town, and the Spanish blueprint for reorganization of Indian communities. However, there were important local variations. The encomienda system did not embrace the important Indian towns; encomiendas were rather interstitial with reference to the Pueblo towns. The encomiendas were all relatively quite small as compared to those in central New Spain. They became small estancias rather than large institutional arrangements and were of no importance by the late 1600s. The number of Spaniards remained small, and the settlers tended to occupy land outside the areas traditionally held by the Indians. Thus pressure on the land was of minor importance, although in some areas, as around Santa Cruz, it was a factor. Almost from the beginning the conflict between civil and ecclesiastical officials was intense, so that church and state became increasingly distinct, rather than progressively unified, in their policy and practice.[8] The most distinctive feature of this first phase was indeed the constant conflict between church and state, in which, interestingly enough, the ecclesiastical officials were more often in the role of extreme oppressors of the Indians than the civil authorities. Aside from the rivalry of civil and church administrations over command of Indian labor, there were differences over the policy of religious replacement. The Franciscan order was in charge of the program of conversion and took a vigorous stand on the suppression of Indian ceremony. Destruction of religious paraphernalia and rigorous suppression of native ceremonials were increasingly emphasized by the Franciscans, while civil authorities usually took a permissive position. Moreover, civil administrators tended to regard the missionary efforts as unnecessarily disruptive and therefore opposed them on the grounds of maintaining civil order. Indeed, the Franciscan program of executing ceremonial leaders led to a concerted rebellion of the Indians in 1680 which resulted in the expulsion of all Spaniards to the southern margin of the Pueblo area at El Paso for some fifteen years.

In the years preceding the crisis of the 1680 revolt the missionaries established themselves in most of the already concentrated Pueblo settlements. "Reduction" was not necessary in the face of the degree of concentration which already characterized Pueblo life. With military aid at their command the missionaries forced Indians to build churches at the margins of their towns. As usual the Indians were required to work by the missionaries without pay, to maintain herds of livestock, and to carry on the basic work of the church. They set up, in accordance with general policy, a town organization with governors and assistants for the purpose of relating the Indians to the civil and ecclesiastical administrations. The Pueblo area was divided into seven districts, each under the jurisdiction of a Spanish alcalde and staff, as well as the missionary head of church administration.

The Indian communities at the beginning of Spanish administration were different from those of the Aztecs. They were politically autonomous seats of local government unlinked by any form of political or military organization. There was no hereditary class of political rulers or priests. There was in fact no class structure based on economic power or possession. Decapitation in any sense was therefore an impossibility. Politico-ecclesiastical incorporation proceeded differently from the way it did in the Valley of Mexico. The missionary or priest achieved no role within any community as a part of a reorganized local government except as an outside official; the local Indian priesthoods continued in existence. To have eliminated them would have required the complete disruption of the whole town population. The towns were not reconstituted units as among the Yaquis, and therefore the missionary was not in a strategic position to assume authority. It was the sense of their failure to change this basic pattern that led the missionaries of the 1600s to attempt to suppress the native religious organization. The civil side of Pueblo town life was subject to the Spanish blueprint, but here again no basic reorganization took place. The Pueblos modified one or two of their existing local government offices, chiefly that of the outside relations, or war chief, so that they became channels for contact and communication with the Spanish alcalde system. The office was called governor, or sometimes cacique. But the holder of the office was peripheral to the basic structure of peace and ceremonial officials.

The second phase of Spanish rule developed after the 1680 Rebellion and extended through the eighteenth century. After the reconquest in 1696, the civil administration became dominant over the ecclesiastics, it being generally recognized that the policy of religious suppression had brought on the revolt. So, the basic structure of the towns changed hardly at all during the century. The repressive policy was not reinstituted. The civil administration had not found tribute very rewarding and paid less and less attention to its collection. The major problem became one of mere survival in the face of the increasing warlike activity stimulated by the Spanish invasion among the more nomadic tribes.[9] The existing means of integration of the Pueblo towns through the go-between position of governor, without further pressure for internal reorganization, was allowed to continue. The declining influence of the missionaries was in part a result of the developing crisis for defense against the nomadic tribes as the civil authorities took hold; in part it was also a result of reduction of the missionary force and the less and less effective contacts between them and the Indians.

Most important as an influence in Spanish-Indian relations

126

were the defense needs of the Spaniards. Both Apaches and Comanches were emerging as a serious threat to the continued holding of the areas by the Spaniards. In this Spaniards and Pueblos had a common cause because settled Pueblo communities, as well as the Spanish towns, were under the same attack. Spanish policy increasingly recognized the need for close alliance with the Pueblos. To this end they encouraged and brought into their military organization all of the Pueblo towns. They distributed horses and firearms to Pueblos and encouraged them to organize their own military units for fighting in conjunction with the Spanish settlers. Pueblo war leaders were given Spanish military titles—such as captain and lieutenant—and command over their own forces. They were also allowed to share in the spoils of war along with the Spanish soldiers. They were never given full equality but were officially recognized as better disciplined than the Spanish settlers. In fact, the Spanish governors held up the Pueblos to the settlers as models of organization and morale. Everything possible was done so that the Pueblos would continue their own organization and share in the fruits of success against the nomadic tribes. Thus the role of the Pueblos as fully recognized auxiliaries developed during the eighteenth century. Interference in their local government decreased both from the ecclesiastical and the civil sides. By the 1790s this partnership was well developed; survival of the island of settled Spaniards and Pueblos was assured.

The overall effect was a remarkable persistence of the Pueblo communities in a form very close to what they had before the coming of the Spaniards. Adaptation of a few roles by the Pueblos constituted the main form of political integration. Their religious organization was little modified and with it the general orientation of Pueblo life. Economic exploitation had been reduced, in part because there was little to be gained, and in part because the Spanish settlements had found their own niche and developed an economic life in this relatively underpopulated area which was independent of the Indians. The incorporation process had resulted in a kind of pluralism which left two distinct cultural systems in operation in the Pueblo country. There was neither a re-forming Indian culture like that of the Yaquis, nor a withdrawal from Spanish involvement as in the case of the Aztecs in the Valley of Mexico.

127

Edward H. Spicer

ASSIMILATION IN THE BAJIO

The region which comprised parts of modern Jalisco, Michoacan, and Guanajuato, together with other areas, seems to have been that part of New Spain in which the cultural assimilation of Indians into colonial Spanish cultural orientations took place on the grandest scale and most rapidly. Just how this came about, process for process, is not fully clear, but Eric Wolf and some others have offered facts which suggest the course of events.[10]

To begin with we know that this region was one of the most completely devastated by the conquest. Nuño de Guzmán seems to have been the model of the destructive conquistador. We read that he laid waste villages, executed people for not revealing secrets about nonexistent gold, and generally swept through the area from east to west as far as Guadalajara, the embodiment of ruthless conquest. By 1541, the wholesale destruction gave rise to a desperate, last-ditch resistance in the Mixton Wars. This meant more destruction. I have no figures which indicate the effects of this phase of conquest on the Indian population. What would seem to have been involved was perhaps greater population decline than in the Valley of Mexico, and in addition the elimination of many, perhaps most, Indian settlements which had long been inhabited. Almost simultaneously two trends were initiated. In the southern, more mountainous part of the region, Father Vasco de Quiroga began work with the intention of rebuilding the wrecked society. His famous system of hospitals or reorganized village communities, based on Sir Thomas More's Utopia, was instituted and affected many Tarascan people, especially in the vicinity of Lake Pátzcuaro and the mountains to the west.[11] However, this affected only a small part of the people of the region. Meanwhile the Spaniards had discovered what turned out to be the largest silver deposit in all of New Spain at Guanajuato. This was to have far-reaching effects on the relations between Indians and Spaniards.

In summary, thousands of Indians displaced by the Guzmán conquest and the Mixton Wars had available, in their immediate vicinity, a reasonably good means of subsistence in the form of wages from the Guanajuato mines and the Spanish settlements that sprang

128

up in the vicinity. Wolf has demonstrated that detribalization proceeded here with unusual rapidity; by about 1800, the proportion of
Indians unaffiliated with a home community was greater than in any
other region of New Spain.[12]

Thus there is indication of a process here quite different from
any of the three already described. It involved the destruction and
desertion of the Indian communities and the consequent displacement of the greater part of the total Indian population during a century and a half. Two kinds of adjustment developed. On the one
hand a minority of a few tens of thousands of Indians were reconstituted in communally administered settlements in predominantly
European patterns of organization and in terms of the cult of the
Virgin. The direction in this rehabilitation program was chiefly
Spanish, through the benevolent management of Father Quiroga.
The program seems to have been confined to the southeast of the
region. The other means of rehabilitation consisted of participation
in the wage-work system which focused around the mines of the
Sierra Madre Occidental. This meant a progressive cultural assimilation on the part of Indians who had lost their territorial roots. The
great majority took this route and became the foundation of Mexico's mestizo population—mixed not only in genetic constitution,
but also in culture, with a predominantly Spanish set of cultural orientations. They came into the Spanish society of New Spain at the
bottom and remained there in large numbers. But as they embraced
wage work and town life, something of a new class began to develop,
especially in the vicinity of Morelia (Valladolid) and Guanajuato.
Indians were moving into the mestizo society generally by the early
1800s.

THE NATURE OF
THE POLITICAL INTEGRATION

We have considered four different varieties of incorporation
processes in New Spain. All contributed to a common result which
consisted of the establishment and maintenance of Spanish political
control over Indians. Each also contributed to the establishment of
different kinds of relations within the whole between Indian com-

munities and the overarching political structure. For the purpose of thinking more clearly about these kinds of integration we might apply categorizing labels to them. For example, it might be said that the incorporation of the Aztecs involved an alienating process, such that the Indians focused on rejecting full participation in the society of New Spain. The Yaquis might be characterized at the end of the colonial period as secessionist in that the process of incorporation led not to a passive alienation from the Spaniards but rather to a militant separatism. The Pueblo integration consisted of an accommodating adjustment within the whole. In the Bajío and adjacent areas the major integrating process involved individual assimilation with an accompanying disintegration of Indian communities. These terms—alienating, secessionist, accommodating, and assimilative—call attention to distinctive results with respect to the relations of Indian entities to the dominant political entity of New Spain. Persisting in an effort to see these varieties of integration from the standpoint of the relations of parts to the dominant society, it would be profitable to explore the prevailing attitudes of dominant society members. I think we might find that labels employed by representatives of the civil administration could be summed up in the following: backward for the Aztecs, barbarian for the Yaquis, cooperative for the Pueblos, and perhaps something like progressive for the Bajío Indians.

These varieties of results in the incorporation processes are not to be thought of as characterizing only the specific situations which we have selected for analysis. I suspect that in various forms and degrees they were to be found throughout New Spain. Probably the alienating variety was the major one in the vicinity of the largest Spanish settlements in the center and much of the southern highlands. But wherever it was important, the assimilative process was also in operation, affecting varying numbers of Indian individuals and communities. The accommodative process was the rarest, I believe, possibly unique to the northern borderlands. The militant separatist process sometimes grew out of alienation and took form under conditions following the colonial period, but foundations for it had been laid during the period of dominance under New Spain.

Consideration of these varieties of incorporation leads to a better understanding of the flexibility and potential for flexibility which characterized the Spanish cultural system. There were different incorporating mechanisms at the disposal of the viceroy and the crown. Besides the colonial administrative hierarchy itself—consisting of two basic parts, the corregimiento network proper and the local government structure—there were also the missionary orders, which varied widely in regard to techniques, and the economic institutions of mines and haciendas. These various mechanisms gained different degrees of autonomy within the whole and met different needs in different demographic and other circumstances. The structural requisites of the Spanish system varied under these different circumstances; incorporating mechanisms fulfilled the specific requisites in ways which contributed effectively to the maintenance of the whole. However, the viceregal government seems to have managed this in no systematic way. There was imperfect orchestration of these various institutional instruments, and hence uniformity in the results with respect to the whole was not achieved.

It must be said, however, that there was remarkable achievement in incorporating, in some fashion, all the varied societies of the Indians into a single political framework. This was accompanied by the laying of certain foundations for the growth of a single cultural system. The basis for this achievement is to be found in the influence in general policy of one of the ideas of Las Casas. This was the conception of the value of the integrity of the Indian community, even though it may seem paradoxical to assert this in the face of the exposition of the processes of alienation and assimilation.

CULTURAL CHANGE IN
THE INDIAN COMMUNITIES

The kind of change which the conditions of the Spanish empire stimulated for three hundred years in the Valley of Mexico with respect to the Indian communities was regressive. That is to say, the Aztec communities moved steadily towards a lower level of integration. The politico-ecclesiastical linkages of local communities with the national entity of the Aztec organization were severed, and a new network replacing the old was not effectively established. The schools for the sons of chiefs were in no sense a functional replacement for the *calpulli* educational system. They were not rooted in the Indian communities but were set up as part of the Spanish system. They did not provide a recruitment mechanism reaching into the communities for higher levels of church or state bureaucracy. In these respects, as well as with regard to the drain on resources through tribute, a wedge was driven between local and national levels preventing integration on Spanish terms. What resulted was a new orientation toward the small-scale group and its maintenance. Capacity for organization became more and more restricted to the small communities. There was sometimes loss of identification even with an entity as large as the cabecera. The system of elders became effective in maintaining this local focus and resisting linkage of a wider sort. Intercommunity organization was so interfered with that rebellion against the Spaniards could not be organized. The whole tendency was towards contraction of the sphere of social action and, with that, contraction of common identification. This was detribalization without new national identification.

In contrast the Yaquis were led to move in the opposite direction. The one-strand linkage with the Spanish empire, almost exclusively through the ecclesiastical organization, resulted in a vitalization of Yaqui society at a new, higher level of integration. The mission community which developed was a synthesis of much smaller communities, the *rancherías*. The Jesuit town became a highly organized and intricately reinforced system. Perhaps its most characteristic institution was the *cofradía*. The intensified utilization of the local resources was highly visible to members of the local communities as they participated in the wider programs of Jesuit mission extension. The new, wider organization was not merely imposed; it involved intensive Yaqui participation, to a large extent on their own terms. The vitalization reached beyond the local town itself, reinforcing the preexisting capacity for tribal organization of warfare, in terms of the new ceremonialism built on Catholic symbolism. The *cofradía* system became an important mechanism of intertown ceremonial cooperation, and the Yaqui tribal sense was intensified. Cultural change among the Yaquis steadily took the course of stimulation of a new intertown entity which began to see itself as distinct from New Spain. The conditions were ripe for a militant separatist movement, which did develop during the nineteenth century.

Developments in the Pueblo area were nearly unique and hence are of relatively lesser interest for understanding the entity of New Spain. The basic effect here was a set of conditions which inhibited any but minor changes. The Pueblo cultural system did not alter in fundamental ways during the whole three hundred years of Spanish rule. The Pueblos remained substantially the same kind of small-scale cultural units that they had been at the time of Coronado. There were shifts in population and the adaptation of some local government offices. There were small adjustments to the economically independent Spanish settler communities. There was indeed the development of new military organization, but this was carried out within the existing Pueblo structure. The Pueblos remained encysted and relatively static within the Spanish cultural system.

I cannot present material indicating the processes of change in the Bajío area with respect to Indian communities. Many disintegrated completely and many that continued for a while lost their populations to the haciendas and city barrios. This was a basic process of the development of mestizo Mexican culture as it took place generally. Our focus is here on the Indian cultures rather than on mestizo culture. Other Indian communities were revitalized to some extent, after disintegration, by the hospitals of Quiroga and similar institutional rebuilding. To a limited degree there must have been processes similar to those that brought about the vitalization of the Yaqui communities. Some communities, such as the Tarascan towns of the Cañada, tended to take the Aztec route of regressive change.

CONCLUSION

To return to the nature of the entity of New Spain as it developed over three hundred years in the region of modern Mexico, it may be said that this political unit came to include, in some kind of working relations, millions of people. This was a remarkable achievement of large-scale reorganization. It did not, however, bring about a uniform higher level of integration of this large population. As we have seen, processes had been set in motion, leading in at least two directions, which were counter to the maintenance of the maximum level of the new integration. On the one hand there was the wide-spread tendency in Indian communities to move toward a lower level of integration than had characterized them before conquest. On the other hand there were tendencies among Indians counter to the soli-darity of the whole political system. A tendency toward separatism had been stimulated which was developing along two lines: nonmili-tant withdrawal in a regressive process, and militant separatism at a new tribal, or national, level.

Thus the New Spain which faced the nineteenth century with its growing domination by mestizos was an entity comprising several different kinds of substructures involving Indians. The assumptions of the new mestizo leadership, which eventually asserted itself, were based essentially on their own experience in the process of rejection of Indian community life and of individual assimilation into the mestizo-oriented towns and cities. The measures they adopted for building and maintaining an overall political system, which could sustain a greater unity than the colonial system, realistically took into account neither of the kinds of separatism which had been stim-ulated. The Indian revolts which racked the new nation during the last half of the century, ranging from the War of the Castes in the south to the Yaqui wars of the north, were continuations of one pro-cess begun in mission and other communities during the colonial era. No means other than forcible breakup of the Indian communities was devised for channeling that process toward wider integration at the level of the Mexican nation. The other process of withdrawal and localization was counter to the whole dominant trend. No concep-tion of Indian-mestizo relations was developed for effectively coun-tering either until well after the 1910 revolution.

NOTES

1— Lewis Hanke, *The Spanish Struggle for Justice in the Conquest of America* (Boston, 1965).

2— Charles Gibson, *The Aztecs Under Spanish Rule: A History of the Indians in the Valley of Mexico, 1519-1810* (Palo Alto, 1964).

3— Ibid., pp. 93-95.

4— Ibid., p. 118.

5— Ibid., p. 127.

6— Edward H. Spicer, ed., *Perspectives in American Indian Culture Change* (Chicago, 1961).

7— Oakah L. Jones, Jr., *Pueblo Warriors and Spanish Conquest* (Norman, Okla., 1966).

8— France V. Scholes, "Church and State in New Mexico, 1610-1650," Historical Society of New Mexico, no. 7 (Albuquerque, 1937).

9— Jones, p. 31-32.

10— Eric R. Wolf, *The Mexican Bajío in the Eighteenth Century, An Analysis of Cultural Integration* (New Orleans, 1955).

11— Silvo A. Zavala, *La "Utopia" de Tomás Moro en la Nueva España* (Mexico, 1937).

12— Wolf, p. 191.

CONTRIBUTORS

DAURIL ALDEN, born in 1926, received his A.B., M.A. and Ph.D. from the University of California at Berkeley. He has had visiting appointments at Columbia University, the University of California at Berkeley, and the University of Michigan and is presently a professor of history at the University of Washington. In 1969 Professor Alden was made a Gulbenkian Foundation Fellow. He is a member of the Board of Editors of *The Hispanic American Historical Review* and has published several articles as well as a book, *Royal Government in Colonial Brazil.*

LEWIS HANKE was born in Oregon City, Oregon, in 1905. He received his Bachelor's and Master's degrees from Northwestern University and his Ph.D. from Harvard in 1936. Professor Hanke has taught at the University of Hawaii, the American University of Beirut, Harvard University, the University of Texas, Columbia University and the University of California at Irvine. In July of 1969 he became Clarence H. and Helen Haring Professor of History at the University of Massachusetts. In addition to several honorary degrees and awards, Professor Hanke was presented the Bartolomé Mitre Medal by the Hispanic Society of America in 1967. He has published many articles and books, including *Bartolomé Arzáns de Orsúa y Vela's History of Potosí, Contemporary Latin America: A Short History,* and *Estudios sobre Fray Bartolomé de Las Casas y sobre la lucha por la justicia en la conquista española de América.*

CONTRIBUTORS

WILBUR R. JACOBS, born in Chicago in 1918, received his education at the University of California in Los Angeles, obtaining his Ph.D. in 1941. He has taught at Johns Hopkins, Stanford, the University of Colorado, the University of Michigan, where he was William L. Clements Library lecturer, and the University of California at Santa Barbara. In 1969 he became a Fulbright lecturer at the Australian National University. Professor Jacobs has been associated with several historical societies, and he is currently a member of the Conference on Peace Research in History. In addition to his many articles he has also published a number of books including *The Historical World of Frederick Jackson Turner* and *Wilderness Politics and Indian Gifts*, and has edited *The Appalachian Indian Frontier*, and *The Paxton Riots and the Frontier Theory*.

EDWARD H. SPICER was born in Cheltenham, Pennsylvania, in 1906. He received his B.A. and M.A. from the University of Arizona and, in 1939, completed his Ph.D. at the University of Chicago. Presently he is professor of anthropology at the University of Arizona. He has also taught at Dillard University in New Orleans and has been a visiting professor at Cornell and the University of California. Professor Spicer has received two fellowships from the Guggenheim Foundation. In addition to several articles, Professor Spicer has also written and edited *Cycles of Conquest, Perspectives in American Indian Culture Change*, and *Pascua, A Yaqui Village in Arizona*.

ALLEN W. TRELEASE was born in Boulder, Colorado, in 1928. He received his A.B. and M.A. from the University of Illinois, and, in 1955, he completed his Ph.D. at Harvard. He has been chairman of the Department of History and Government at Wells College and, since 1967, professor of history at the University of North Carolina at Greensboro. Professor Trelease's articles have appeared in the *Mississippi Historical Review* and the *Journal of Southern History*. He is also the author of a book, *Indian Affairs in Colonial New York: The Seventeenth Century*.

MASON WADE, born in 1913 in New York City, received his M.A. from McGill University in 1953, an LL.D. from the University of New Brunswick in 1957, and a D.Litt. from the University of Ottawa in 1963. He has been a Guggenheim Fellow and is a former president of the Canadian Historical Association. From 1963 to 1965, Professor Wade was chairman of the American section of the Joint Committee of American and Canadian Historical Associations. He is presently senior professor of history at the University of Western Ontario. Among his many books and articles are *Francis Parkman*, *The French Canadian Outlook*, and *Canadian Dualism*, which he edited.

139